Yesterday's Doll

Cora Taylor

D0963623

AN
APPLE
PAPERBACK

SCHOLASTIC INC.
New York Toronto London Auckland Sydney

*This book is lovingly dedicated
to the memory of my grandmother
SARAH ANN SHEARER KALBFLEISCH
who came to the Carlton District in 1882
carrying a doll named Jessie*

First published in Canada by Western Producer Prairie Books as *The Doll*.

ISBN 0-590-43208-7

12 11 10 9 8 7 6 5 4 3 2 1   0 1 2 3 4 5/9

PRINTED IN CANADA   11

First Scholastic printing, January 1990

1

The doll's name was Jessie. Not Jessica which was elegant, or Jessamine which was splendid, or even Jess which had a certain dignity, but Jessie. It seemed a very common-sounding name for such an unusual doll. A cow-like name. It reminded Meg of Bossie. Not at all appropriate, but then names seldom are. Take her own for instance. Meg. Nothing to it. Just plain Meg.

She was always being asked, "What's Meg short for?" And she had to admit that it wasn't short for Megan which had an old-fashioned distinction, or Margaret which was refined—like a princess—but that it was just, simply, Meg.

She lay in bed, not moving. Staring at the china doll on the top of the oak dresser. Not really a dresser like hers at home; Grandma called this a highboy and it was tall. Meg couldn't have reached the doll even if she'd wanted to.

"What's Meg short for?" a new teacher would ask and some jerk behind her would say: "Because she forgot to grow!" Then everybody would laugh and Meg would wish she could shrink right out of sight.

She didn't care that she couldn't reach the doll but it reminded her of the question she'd been afraid to ask all the time she'd been sick with rheumatic fever. "Will I stop growing altogether now?" She hadn't asked, of course.

Someone might have laughed at her. Still, being so sick for such a long time had to have some effect—didn't it? The thought of going through life as a small ten-year-old was more than she could stand.

She might have asked her mother on the drive out from Saskatoon today. It would have been a good time. Except that Mum had been acting strange. Explaining things. "Your father couldn't come with us because he has an appointment . . . something he has to do . . . somewhere he has to go . . ." Meg remembered feeling insulted. Did her mother think she didn't know the meaning of the word appointment? Now, thinking back on it, it had been almost as if Mum were talking to herself. At the time it hadn't bothered Meg that her dad couldn't come and she hadn't thought anything of it, but after the explanation she'd begun to wonder. Her parents had been acting funny lately. They hadn't come to visit her together at the hospital the last few weeks she'd been in. And since she'd been home they seemed to be avoiding each other. She couldn't remember Dad being away so much before. There were so many little things and when Meg put them together . . .

They hadn't told her anything yet, very careful not to upset her when she'd been so sick. Didn't they realize a person, even a very short, sick person, could hear? Late at night, with the bedroom door closed, a person could wake up and hear if the other people yelled loud enough.

Now her mother's leave-of-absence time was up at the office and Meg had come to visit her Grandma Cameron so that she could recuperate and have someone there all day to look after her. Meg didn't mind the visit part. Grandma Grace was one of her favourite people. "Spoils you rotten," her dad said.

It was nice too, getting out of the city into a small town where everybody knew who you were. She loved the old Cameron house, full of shiny old furniture, squeaky but comfortable wicker chairs and frilly curtains. The trouble was that if she was here, at Grandma Cameron's, she wouldn't be there. At home. So now her parents would have more chances to fight. At least when she was around they didn't, not if they knew she was listening. When she was there they weren't able to do more than argue a bit. Usually they were polite . . . a fierce kind of politeness that made Meg wonder why manners had been invented at all.

Meg sighed. Maybe it was too late already; she was almost sure it was. This family didn't hide things very well. Their hugs gave them away. Her dad hugged her for a long time before she got in the car and then turned away too quickly. When they got here her Grandma had hugged her too tight and then let go fast, pretending she shouldn't squeeze a sick girl so hard. If her mother said good-bye and buried her face in Meg's neck the way she had the day they found out she had rheumatic fever and had to go into hospital, Meg would know the worst.

She sat up, listening. Downstairs her mother was having tea in Grandma's warm kitchen and even with the bedroom door open Meg couldn't hear a word. She crept out of bed. Maybe if she sat on the top step of the big staircase she could hear better. But before she was able to sit down her mother was coming up the stairs.

"You shouldn't be out of bed, Meg. You'll catch a chill."

"Do you want anything, dear?" came her grandmother's voice.

Meg tried desperately to think of something she wanted. Grandma had left a glass of juice on the night table and she hadn't touched it so she couldn't ask for another. She'd already told them she wasn't hungry. She blurted the first thing that came into her head.

"How did you know I was out of bed?"

Her mother actually laughed. "Aaah, the family secret is out!"

Grandma laughed too and Meg was relieved that she didn't have to think up an excuse for being there. They'd be reminiscing in a minute and she always liked listening to them do that.

Back in bed, with her mother at the foot and Grandma fluffing pillows, Grandma explained.

"It's very simple Meg honey, but it used to drive your mother crazy when she was a child and tried to sneak out of bed. There's a squeaky board on the landing."

"Third from the front, if I recall correctly."

"And children in the family have always wondered how their parents knew they were out of bed."

"Of course when we figured it out we never told the younger ones . . . let them catch on for themselves."

Meg was surprised to notice how relaxed her mother's face had become.

Meg suddenly felt very tired and her feet had grown cold when she was out of bed. She really didn't feel that much better. She closed her eyes a moment.

"Poor Meg, that drive played you out." Her mother glanced at her watch. "Look at the time. I've still got to get back to Saskatoon tonight."

She went over to the bed and squeezed Meg's hand.

Meg squeezed back. She noticed the tired, sad look was back on her mother's face. She realized it had been there a long time but she hadn't really noticed it until now, when it had vanished for a little while. I suppose I've been too sick to notice, she thought.

Now her mother bent over the bed holding her close. "Poor Meg," she said again and buried her face in Meg's neck.

When she straightened up she said the usual 'Get better' and 'See you soon' but Meg couldn't answer. It was all she could do to muster a wobbly smile as her mother went out the door.

The front door closed a few moments later and Meg could hear Grandma coming up the stairs. She turned her face to the wall and blinked hard to get rid of the tears.

4

Meg heard the door open behind her and felt Grandma brush softly against the bed before she turned her head to see the caring face bent over her.

"Are you all right, love? Warm enough? I've brought you a hot water bottle."

She had too, an old red rubber bottle covered in a kind of tea cosy Grandma had crocheted out of fluffy peach-coloured wool.

"My feet are ... a bit cold," Meg admitted.

The soft warmth was welcome. Just right. Meg felt herself begin to relax. She realized she'd been trembling inside. She lay still, unmoving, letting the warmth work its way up from her toes.

Grandma unfolded the comforter from the foot of the bed, tucked it around Meg and straightened up. Meg watched her, loving the familiar short curly hair and the track suits she always wore because 'they're comfortable'. Today's had a Save the Whales motto.

"Why, I've forgotten to give you Jessie. I brought her up this morning especially. You can't be a proper invalid without the Invalid Doll!"

Meg knew about Jessie. The doll had come west in a Red River cart and been through the Riel Rebellion. Jessie had belonged to Meg's Great-Great-Grandmother Shearer and was over a hundred years old. She was kept in the cedar chest that had been great-great-grandmother's hope chest, and children, even Grandma Grace when she was a child, only got to hold her if they were sick.

"That doll has gone through typhoid fever, the 1918 'flu epidemic when my Aunt Pearl almost died, and goodness knows how many other diseases. Even your mother's whooping cough." Grandma laughed. "We've always said that Jessie was loaded with the germs of generations but the children always got better so I suppose she didn't contaminate them."

Meg didn't bother to tell Grandma she was too old for dolls now and that she hadn't played with her Barbie dolls for months, well weeks, anyway. Besides, Jessie wasn't like any doll Meg had ever had.

Her face was exquisite. Smooth white porcelain skin. Too white for any pretense at being real skin but somehow right for her. The cheeks were delicately tinted pink and, despite the contrast with the white face, the pink was blended so that it faded into Jessie's face, like the shading Meg had seen on the petals of some of Grandma's roses. But it was the eyes . . .

"Could I get you anything else? Some hot, nourishing broth?"

They both smiled. 'Hot nourishing broth' was a family joke. At least the phrase was a family joke; Grandma meant the broth part. Meg had already had a cup of it when she first arrived.

"Your Grandma thinks that all the problems of the world can be solved by two things," Meg's mother once told her, " 'hot nourishing broth' for children and a 'nice cup of tea' for adults."

She might be right about the tea part, Meg thought, remembering the change in her mother's face after tea with Grandma.

"Maybe a little."

When Grandma disappeared down the stairs Meg began to really examine the doll. It was the first time she had ever been allowed to hold it. Now, a genuine invalid at last, she moved her fingers over Jessie's shiny black hair. It wasn't hair at all, of course, just bumps like waves on her head painted to look like hair. Meg shut her eyes and ran her hand over Jessie's head. No, it didn't feel a bit like hair. She opened her eyes again and looked right into Jessie's eyes.

Every time she confronted those eyes, Meg felt strange, but she couldn't actually define the feeling. As though she were trespassing—embarrassed because she'd been caught staring impolitely? She wasn't sure. Jessie's expression was one of imperturbable dignity, as though she'd seen everything and nothing could alarm her. But there was something else . . . something Meg couldn't quite identify . . .

"There now, here's your broth dear."

Meg took the cup. She was feeling hot now, not cold, and didn't really want a hot drink but she felt rather mean to have made Grandma go down to the kitchen to fix it. She noticed Grandma was puffing a little from the climb up the stairs, so she drank enough to justify the trip and lay back.

Grandma was tucking the covers around her again, straightening Jessie's china arms on top of the covers.

"You know, when I was little, I used to think the reason Jessie was so white was because she never got out into the sun. That's why my sisters and I called her the Invalid Doll. We always recovered from our illnesses and were healthy again but she never did." She stared thoughtfully at the doll. "I really believed that . . . that there was some illness . . . something about her . . ."

Grandma's voice trailed off and then she seemed to shake herself and briskly finished tucking the blankets around Meg.

"She smells as though she's been out . . . in a forest."

"That's the cedar from the chest where she's spent the last eighty years. Does it remind you of a forest? It reminds me of mothballs and things stored away."

Grandma's hand had gone automatically to Meg's forehead. It was a familiar gesture of her mother's. Meg supposed that it was another of the family traditions, checking your child for a fever, but to Meg it was somehow tender . . . like a caress.

"You're a bit hot, love."

"I'm tired after all, I guess," Meg said, closing her eyes and curling up on her side.

Grandma's lips brushed her forehead. "Then you get

some sleep, there's a good girl. I'll come in and check on you again before I go to bed."

Meg opened her eyes.

"Poor Invalid Doll," she said, but it was hard to feel sorry for Jessie face to face with those determined china features. The eyes still bothered her. Almost as if they held something . . . as if they were haunted.

Meg didn't like looking at those eyes anymore. She examined the tattered dress Jessie wore. An old-fashioned lady's dress with high neck and tightly fitted bodice, Meg could see where once the skirt had been rows and rows of ruffles made of some soft brown flowered material. Now the cloth had fallen to shreds with age but instead of looking ragged, it looked soft and gauzy, like a ballerina's dress. Meg pulled the doll to her. The stuffed body was soft too, but Jessie was not really a cuddly comforting kind of doll. Still, the china face was lovely and cool against her own. It felt just right.

Meg closed her eyes and breathed the cedar smell. It wasn't heavy like mothballs at all, she thought; in fact it was quite fresh, like trees and grass. She felt a cool breeze on her face and opened her eyes to bright sunshine.

She was on a hillside. Below her a clump of poplar trees had just begun to change colour although the breeze had some of the softness of summer in it. She was holding the doll tightly in her arms.

2

Meg blinked her eyes. The brilliance was a shock after the dimly lit bedroom. So was the fresh breeze. She looked down at Jessie; at least there was something familiar to cling to. But Jessie was somehow different. The same impassive china face, the same strange blue eyes. Then Meg knew what it was. Jessie was no longer dressed in the ragged dress and the heavy denim petticoat. She was wearing a plain blue dress of some very heavy material. There was a lot of it. Flannel, like the old sheets Meg's Grandma used on the beds in the wintertime, but heavier and dark blue. Then she realized it wasn't just Jessie's dress, it was hers too. She looked herself over. What a funny outfit! The dress was miles long and she was wearing long stockings. Worse still, they were knitted and the ribs itched in the warm sun. She stuck out her foot for a better look. Boots. Laced-up ankle boots. Badly scuffed ones at that. Good grief!

Meg sat down and scratched her knee. It was the first time she'd ever felt itchy in a dream. But then you weren't supposed to remember dreams very clearly when you woke up. Maybe she'd been itchy before but couldn't remember.

She could hear a thudding sound and noticed move-

9

ment in the trees below. One tall straight poplar was shaking rhythmically as though it was being struck again and again. As she watched, it tilted and crashed to the ground. Someone was chopping trees. Of course.

Just then a woman in a long dark dress appeared and, cupping her hands to her mouth, called, "Mooooorag!"

Meg looked around. There was nobody else in sight. The strange lady must be calling her. She got to her feet and began walking down the hill. The woman saw her and, waving, turned back, scooping up a small child as she disappeared into the trees.

Meg paused. It looked as though the woman was calling her. It sounded like her name but she'd never been here before or seen the woman or child before in her life, she was sure of that.

She reminded herself that this was, after all, a dream, and hugging Jessie a little tighter than necessary, she walked quickly down the hill to investigate.

Once Meg was through the bushes and into the clearing on the other side, she realized she was in the midst of a family at a campground. But it was a camp like no other she'd ever seen in her life. True, there was a campfire with something in a large black pot simmering on it but that was the only thing that looked remotely familiar. There were the woman and child she'd already seen. Beyond them, neatly trimming branches off the fallen poplar tree with an axe was a tall bearded man. And the costumes. How strange! The lady and the little girl were wearing long dresses of the same dark blue material she wore herself. Even the man's shirt looked to be made of it although he did have on black trousers that didn't fit very well at the waist and were held up by striped suspenders.

Meg backed nervously away, wondering how soon she could turn tail and run. Perhaps if she moved quietly into the bushes she could just disappear. She turned to go only to be confronted by one of the biggest animals she'd ever seen. A bull? A buffalo? It had longer horns that any buffalo she'd ever seen—stuffed or in picture books.

She shrieked and turned to run back into the clearing when a boy came out from behind the beast, patted it and shook his head, laughing at her. "Morag, you've got to get used to the oxen. You know Buck wouldn't hurt a fly."

It looked as though this might be true. The huge beast had not even seemed to notice her, intent as he was on wrapping his long pink tongue around some coarse grass growing in among the young poplar. But why did this boy act like he knew her? And who was Morag?

"Morag, lass," called the woman, looking straight at Meg, "watch Lizzie for a wee while so that I can make some fresh bannock for supper. She seems bent on running over to Papa and having a tree fall on her head." With that she pushed the toddler towards Meg and turned towards a wagon that seemed to be top-heavy with bags and boxes.

"But I'm not . . ." Meg began.

"Bannock's not as fine as your scones, Mother, but it's better than that hardtack in the barrel!" The boy gave Meg's hair a little yank as he went by her. "Quit gaping, sister dear, and mind the baby for Mother."

Three impulses struck Meg simultaneously. 'The creep, how dare he!' was the first one, followed by 'How could he when I've just had my hair cut the shortest it's ever been?' Both those thoughts were wiped out by the sight of a tiny dark blue form running right in the direction of the chopping. Meg dashed forward and scooped up the child.

"Dessie Doll," lisped the little girl, wiggling to grab the doll as Meg struggled to keep a grip on both child and doll. "Moog!" she chortled, throwing fat arms around Meg's neck.

That's the closest anyone's come to my real name, thought Meg as she set the child down and tried to pry the chubby fingers from around her braid. Her braid! She felt her head. She had braids all right, long ones. That's what that jerk who'd had the nerve to call her sister, had yanked. At least the hair was the same colour as hers. I wonder if I even look like me, she mused. It was a frightening thought.

"Geordie," said the woman, "would you go down to the crick and fetch me a little more water?" She paused her kneading in the big wooden bowl to point to a wooden bucket nearby. "Morag, you can go along but watch Lizzie doesn't fall down the bank."

Meg took the baby's hand and followed. She stayed at the top as the boy scrambled down the bank to where the stream formed a quiet pool of clear water. It was still and smooth like a mirror. Meg was almost afraid to look but just as frightened not to know. There were the long brown braids and funny-looking blue dress, and the chubby face of the strange little girl. But in the midst of the pool just before the bucket hit the water disturbing its glassy surface, a face, pale and frightened but familiar. Her own. A wave of relief swept over her.

Just before supper a tall gangly boy older than Geordie appeared carrying two rabbits he had snared. Everyone congratulated him.

"That's grand work. Rabbit stew will be a change from the everlasting beans and bannock." Geordie was beaming.

"Dinna complain, lad. The Lord provides well for us." The man called Papa smiled. "Did you gather up all your snares? We'll not waste them by leaving them behind."

"Nor waste the Lord's wee creatures by killing them for nought," added the mother.

Meg turned away from the limp bodies of the rabbits. Much as she hated beans, she wasn't sure she could eat rabbit stew, not when she'd seen the poor things freshly killed like that.

They sat round on logs with their tin plates full of beans and the bannock still hot from the pan. Meg watched as

12

even little Lizzie bowed her head when the man they called Papa began a long prayer. She realized she was tired. Do you get tired in dreams? Meg wondered. She wasn't paying as much attention until she heard her new name mentioned.

". . . and thank Thee for bringing our Morag safely through her sickness to be well once again. Amen."

At that they all raised their eyes and looked at her with such tenderness she could almost feel it. Even that jerk Geordie looked as though she mattered. She lowered her eyes, embarrassed. So I've been sick here too, she thought. I've got two big brothers and a little sister.

Later, as she lay on the ground with quilts piled below and above her, and the woman came to kiss her good night, she could hardly keep her eyes open.

"Morag lass, you'd better let me put your doll safely in the wagon for fear Lizzie wakes before you do and does it some harm."

Meg clung to the doll. "Please, no . . ." She could not explain that it was the only familiar thing she had. "Please . . ."

The woman smiled tenderly. "I'll move it after you're asleep . . . before Papa and I turn in ourselves." Lips brushed Meg's forehead and she could hear the man and woman talking by the fire.

"She really loves that doll Granny Shearer gave her before we left Peterborough County. She's not had it out of her arms all day."

The voices droned on. Beside her Lizzie stirred in her sleep. Meg buried her face in Jessie's dress. It didn't seem to smell quite the same, still woodsy but stale perhaps? Maybe a *little* like mothballs after all.

It seemed she was awake instantly, but there was a soft bed under her and a ceiling above instead of the hard ground and starry sky. Jessie was far away on the other side of the bed facing the wall and Grandma was bending over her smiling in the morning sunshine.

"Well, Meg, you've slept the clock around. That's the way to get better!"

3

Meg smiled up at Grandma. She was glad to be back in the familiar bed but she didn't feel as if she'd been asleep that long. The dream had seemed so real. She raised her hand to her head and was relieved, almost surprised, to feel her own short hair. Jessie lay face down in a tumble of blankets. The doll was back in her tattered dress. It was only a dream after all.

"Would you like breakfast in bed or do you feel like coming down and sitting in the kitchen with me?"

Meg loved that kitchen. It had orange gingham curtains with ruffles along the top that let in lots of sunshine. She even liked the matching quilted covers that Grandma made for the toaster and the teapot. Not the sort of thing her mother would dream of having in her kitchen. Hers had hanging plants and baskets everywhere.

Meg remembered her father saying Grandma Grace would stick a cosy on the cat if he'd hold still long enough! She almost laughed out loud at the thought of Old Possum wearing an orange gingham blanket like a horse, with perhaps a little ruffled tea cosy hat to match. Come to think of it she hadn't seen the old rascal since she arrived. Might as well go down for breakfast. She was hungry for a change.

Grandma had her housecoat ready to slip on and, as Meg put her arm in, there was the hand on her forehead and then Grandma was giving her a quick hug. "That's my brave girl," she said in a strange soft voice.

There it was again. Something was definitely up. Something bad and Meg didn't need three guesses.

She held onto the bannister as she went down the stairs, surprised that she felt so stiff and had to walk slowly.

Old Possum was curled up on one of the orange gingham cushions with the sun streaming in on his thick grey coat. He showed his usual enthusiasm for Meg. He didn't move. Just arched his neck for her to pat. Even if she could have, Meg would not have picked him up; he weighed a ton and did not appreciate being moved when he got himself comfortable.

"We're a pair," Grandma always said. "Not as frisky as we used to be."

"Hey Poss! How come you didn't come and sleep with me like you usually do when I'm here?"

"He was up there this morning." Grandma looked puzzled. "And he does claim squatter's rights on that bed . . . especially when you're here. Perhaps he's getting too old . . ."

Meg managed to drink her orange juice and eat most of poached egg on toast that was her usual breakfast at Grandma's.

It was lovely and warm in the bright kitchen; it made her feel as if she was wrapped in cotton wool, floating and safe, the way she used to think it would be to sit on a cloud when she was little.

Grandma was finishing her coffee and studying a pattern book. She was wearing a track suit Meg's father had brought back from one of his trips to Toronto. It was navy blue and said The Tower of London with the initials ROM underneath. When Meg had asked what they stood for he'd told her, Rosie O'Malley.

"Didn't I ever tell you about Rosie O'Malley, one of the most famous prisoners the Tower of London ever had?"

Meg never knew when her father was going to tell one of his tall tales. Sometimes they were so good she almost believed him.

"She was Henry the Eighth's seventh wife." He lowered his voice to a whisper. "Of course, they never mention her in the history books because she was Irish!"

Usually, just when Meg was beginning to wonder if it was all true, her mother would stop laughing long enough to break in, "Mark, stop it! She'll be getting mixed up in school and believe Henry the Eighth actually had seven wives."

Sometimes Meg asked him the same questions again and again just to lead him on. She remembered that the next time she'd asked what ROM stood for he'd said Rosie O'Malley again, but this time she was a daring jailbreaker who'd swum up the Thames and rescued Sir Walter Raleigh from the Tower of London and then they'd gone to Virginia and founded the O'Malley-Raleigh Tobacco Company. Meg smiled at the memory. Then she remembered he hadn't told her one of those silly stories lately and she sighed.

"Don't tell me you're tired already love? Do you want to lie down for a bit?"

Meg didn't feel like moving, but it would be nice to be back snuggling down in bed with Jessie. At last she was able to get up, although her feet and legs didn't seem to belong to her at all. She had to order them along. Up the stairs, holding onto the bannister *and* Grandma's arm this time.

There was Jessie lying on the bed staring at her. Meg began to climb into bed, stopped and stared back at the doll.

"Dear me, I should have straightened this bed while you were up." Grandma tried to reach past Meg to pull at the covers. Meg didn't move. "Meg, honey, you're in my way. Is something wrong?"

"Nnnoo . . . no . . . I don't think so . . ." Meg moved over and sat in the chair by the dresser. Dolls don't move, she thought, even dolls that stare at you as if they knew something you didn't. Even dolls that look smug, the way Jessie was looking now.

Grandma propped the doll up in the corner by the pillow as she began pulling the bottom sheet tight across the mattress, flicking the blankets so that they fell back smooth and neat. The china-blue eyes looked squarely at Meg. Determined.

Meg looked right back at her. Staring too.

Grandma had finished. She drew back the covers and turned to Meg, looking a little startled at Meg's expression. "Are you sure you're all right? No pain anywhere, is there?"

Meg pulled her eyes away from the doll's, feeling dazed. What was the matter with her? She felt as if she'd been having an argument. With a doll of all things! She laughed and gave Grandma a little hug as she went to climb into bed. "I'm fine . . ."

Grace Cameron looked thoughtfully at Meg. She prided herself on being the practical sort. And she was not a worrier. She had to keep reminding herself of that where this favourite granddaughter was concerned. Especially now. Meg was such a quiet type. Never making a fuss. Hardly letting on how she felt when something happened. And yet her grandmother knew Meg cared. It made it even more important now, when Meg's life was going to change so much, that Grandma Grace remain the same. She straightened her shoulders. She was grateful that Meg would have this time away while Mark and Janet sorted things out. She looked down at Meg lying there, her face peaceful and relaxed. Quite a contrast to the doll beside her. Jessie's expression was anything but relaxed. It was relentless, Grace Cameron thought. Implacable.

She remembered the feeling the doll had given her as a child. The staring eyes had always made her a bit uneasy, as if the doll were judging her. Making her feel she'd failed somehow. As if she was not the child Jessie wanted her to be.

It made her feel a bit silly. Even this morning that childhood feeling had been so strong she almost hadn't taken the doll out for Meg. She'd finally done it because she felt that right now Meg needed all the reminders of family and security she could get. After all, the tradition of the Invalid Doll was—well, it was just that. Tradition.

She looked back at Meg. Now, she thought, if I hurry, I can get a bit of weeding done before I'm needed again. Nothing like getting out in the garden. I expect the tomatoes could stand watering. She tiptoed quickly out.

Meg lay there, her eyes closed. She heard Grandma leave. Suddenly she didn't feel very much like sleeping. She was aware of the doll. Without opening her eyes or turning her head, Meg could feel the staring eyes.

This is ridiculous, she thought. But she couldn't ignore it. "All right, Jessie," she said, sitting up, "you're going over there, in the dresser drawer for a while." She threw back the covers and the doll toppled forward and lay face down in a sad-looking heap.

Meg picked her up. Painted eyes. As blue as the prairie sky in her dream. Clear and honest, with no threat in them at all. Meg smiled. Jessie *was* comforting to hold.

She suddenly felt drowsy after all. She cuddled down in bed with the doll and closed her eyes . . .

And opened them to a blue sky and the face of Jerk Geordie grinning down at her.

"Rise and shine, sleepyhead. Mother says to tell you breakfast is almost ready. Must be nice to be a pampered lay-a-bed!"

"Oooh . . ." Meg groaned and sat up. She *was* stiff.

Somebody small ran towards her. Lizzie, fully dressed

and ready for anything, threw herself at Meg, knocking her back down on the quilts, arms tight around her neck.

"Moooog," she said between the wet kisses. "Up?" she said, chubby face inches from Meg's own.

Up, my foot! thought Meg, as if I could move at all with this solid little body parked on my chest. She rolled over giving Lizzie a hug and wondering if dreams usually came in installments. This dream was almost too realistic. She had felt the wind knocked out of her when Lizzie landed. Maybe it's Poss finally coming to sleep with me, sitting on my chest for a minute. At least she didn't feel quite so strange this time. She knew who some of the characters in the dream were. Not as well as they seemed to know her, of course. She tried to untangle herself.

"Dessie Doll," crowed Lizzie, letting go and making a grab for the doll.

There was Jessie all right. Meg had somehow rolled over her. There was the doll in the blue flannel dress. Staring at her. What was the expression in those china-blue eyes? Meg wondered . . . Knowing?

"Lizzie, don't be too rough on Morag, she's been sick." The lady they called Mother lifted the toddler away from Meg. "I let you sleep. It takes time to get over the fever." Meg felt the familiar gesture of a hand on her forehead. The mother was kneeling beside her folding up quilts. She picked up the doll.

"Och, I thought I put your doll away last night. Did you get up and bring it from the wagon? I thought you were sound asleep all this while, lass."

Meg didn't answer. She felt like saying, 'Listen, lady, this is a dream. How do I know how things happen? You think you're confused, you should be in my shoes!' But she didn't say anything, just looked down at her feet. She was in those itchy stockings again and there were the scuffed boots waiting to be put on and the dress the lady was handing her. The same one as yesterday; she obviously was supposed to get dressed now. Good grief! She had a lot of clothes on already: a white cotton slip, long pants (were these what were called pantaloons or bloomers?), and those stockings. She scratched her leg and thought without surprise, 'This obviously isn't the kind of dream where pinching yourself would make any difference.'

"Hurry along now, Morag," said the lady, taking Lizzie's hand. "Papa's going to start prayers."

They were all sitting on the logs when she got there, heads bowed. Prayers in the morning *and* at night, thought Meg. This time the man called Papa read from a big leather Bible all about manna in the wilderness.

Whatever manna was, what they had was oatmeal porridge. The kind Grandma usually made for herself. Meg didn't like it much unless it was covered with brown sugar, and you let that melt so that it looked like syrup. Jerk Geordie was pouring something out of a big jug onto his porridge. It looked like syrup.

"Want some molasses, Morag?"

Molasses! Yuck! "No thanks." Meg took a spoonful of the oatmeal and forced it down.

"Do you think you'll get the new axle for the cart made today, Papa?" asked the older boy, the rabbit snarer, whose name Meg didn't know yet.

Geordie still held the jug towards her. "Pass it to Archy then ..."

Meg stifled a giggle. So the other brother's name was Archy. Except Jerk Geordie said it 'Errchee', sort of like a sneeze. She handed along the jug and the older boy took it. His smile was friendly. Kind. I always wanted an older brother, Meg thought suddenly.

"... Shorty," Geordie finished.

Meg glared at him. A *much* older brother, she amended to herself.

"Let us hope so ... we may even be able to make a start by noon. Five miles would bring us that much closer to Fort Carlton and the homestead."

Meg turned away from Geordie's mocking grin. Now she might be able to learn the purpose of this strange camping trip. Archy was looking worried.

"If we don't break down again. It'll be a whole new Red River cart by the time we get to the homestead. We've replaced two spokes on one wheel, four on the other, new pegs for the axle and now . . ."

"What about all the pieces of rawhide I've had to cut?" interrupted Jerk Geordie, ". . . and the axle socket so that the wood doesn't wear out?"

"Aye, it may be all new when we get there, but at least we'll get there. We can make all the parts we need on the way. Where would we be if we needed metal parts replaced with no smithy nearby? That's the beauty and the curse of the wonderful Red River cart, lad."

He got up and took his plate over to the mother, setting it carefully beside her, his hand resting briefly on her shoulder. "A fine breakfast Hannah." She smiled up at him, a funny crinkly smile that Meg thought looked rather familiar, though she didn't know why.

Archy and Geordie followed their father exactly, taking the bowls and stacking them inside their father's. Meg thought Jerk Geordie was even trying to walk like his father.

Meg quickly dumped the rest of her porridge under a rosebush when no one was looking, picked up the bowl Lizzie had abandoned and brought the plates over to the woman.

She smiled at Meg—that smile again! "We'll wash them as soon as the kettle's hot. Run after Geordie and get him to help you see if there are any eggs in the crates. We don't want them broken when we start to travel again."

Meg didn't like the idea of talking to the jerk but she did as she was told. To her amazement, there behind the wagon were three crates full of chickens that had been unloaded onto the grass. The hens were poking their heads out between the slats pecking at the grass and berries on the rose bushes. Geordie undid one of the crates and slid his hand inside.

"Here's one! See if there's any in that crate, Morag."

Meg bent down trying to peer through the slats between the legs of the chickens. She realized that they were not packed in the crates too tightly and there was some straw at the back of each crate. It looked like two eggs in this one. "Two here," she said. She was afraid he was going to suggest that she reach in and get them out, but he just handed her the egg he'd gathered and undid the other wooden fastener while she crouched down to look in the last crate. There were two eggs in that one too.

Geordie was elated and she felt rather pleased herself as she held the still-warm eggs. She made a little bowl with her skirt, the way she'd seen Grandma do with an apron. It surprised her that she did it naturally, without thinking.

"Five eggs! Mother will be pleased! These poor biddies sometimes don't lay any eggs at all for days, they get shaken up so when the cart lurches along. There'll be an egg for Papa's breakfast, an egg for each of us if this keeps up!"

He busied himself filling earthenware dishes for the chickens, some with water, some with grain. Meg watched for a minute and then, walking carefully, she took the eggs back down the path.

Geordie was right about the eggs. The woman was so delighted Meg felt as if she'd really done something, helping to find them. They were carefully placed in a woven basket that looked a lot like the willow-wand baskets her mother bought at the craft shop.

After she had helped wash the dishes and pack them into a big box in the wagon, she had intended to take Lizzie to pick some wildflowers, but then she yawned and the mother insisted that she climb into the wagon where all the quilts had been piled to make a bed. It did look inviting and soon she and Jessie were curled up, lulled by the wind in the poplars and occasional bird song.

It didn't seem as if she had slept long when she heard the noise of a car.

4

It seemed to Meg in her sleep that a car was the last thing she should be hearing but it sounded familiar. She opened her eyes. Of course – she'd been dreaming about ox teams and Red River carts.

She pushed Jessie aside and hurried to the window, blinking a little in the bright afternoon sunlight. She hadn't slept very long after all. And it was Saturday. She kept getting the days mixed up since she'd been sick.

She looked down at the familiar car. There was her mother getting out on the passenger side, her father climbing out of the other door. They'd come to visit her together! She grabbed her housecoat. No, she'd go to the bathroom and brush her hair first, then go down and surprise them.

She brushed her teeth, then washed her face and brushed her hair. That would give them enough time to get settled in the kitchen with Grandma. She'd tiptoe down. Which board was it that creaked? . . . Third from the front her mother had said.

She could hear the voices in the kitchen, indistinctly at first, just the odd word . . .

". . . civilized thing to do . . . don't want to hurt her . . . want her to understand . . . love her . . ." Her parents' voices. Jumbled.

Grandma's voice: ". . . seems to be sleeping well, but still . . . Mark, Janet, do what you think is best . . ."

Meg was just outside the kitchen door now. She could hear her mother clearly. "We've talked it over Mother . . . and we've decided . . ."

Meg knew she did not want to hear what they had decided. She burst through the door.

"I heard the car . . ." she said. And then she just stood there realizing that for the first time in her life she didn't know which one to run to first because for the first time it really mattered. She would be making a choice and she didn't want to. So she just stood there. And the smile that she'd worn ever since she saw them getting out of the car died on her face.

Her legs felt wobbly. Grandma was closest. Meg turned towards the comforting track suit and held on. She could feel messages being sent behind her back. Grandma shaking her head. Then her father lifting her to the window seat, while her mother piled the gingham cushions behind her back.

"Hey Meg baby!" Her father's face was sad, the lines around his eyes deeper than she remembered. "I didn't know you were still so shaky . . ."

"I told you she needed to rest and get better . . ." Her mother's hand was on her forehead. Meg didn't have to look at her to know that all the lines she'd grown in her face lately would still be there.

Grandma was at the stove with the kettle, filling the teapot. "Tea'll be ready in a minute. Meg, would you like some . . ."

". . . hot nourishing broth?" finished Meg. And somehow then they were laughing, all together. Meg shut her eyes, hoping to hold the moment, knowing deep down that, even if they didn't tell her on this visit, she already knew.

So they drank their tea and she drank her broth and out of the corner of her eye she caught her father looking at her so tenderly it seemed as if his face would break, though when she looked at him he'd smile. And her mother looked at her so sad and concerned that Meg wished they hadn't come because it was all just too much. Too sad. And if it weren't for Grandma, bustling around, bringing cookies instead of crackers to go with the broth and then nearly sitting on Possum, Meg was sure she would have run away and cried. Except that she didn't know if she *could* run anywhere just then.

Finally the visit was over. Her father carried her upstairs, though she was big to be carried and he hadn't done it for years. She was just grateful to see the bed. It seemed safe—like a hideout. She felt she never wanted to leave it again, as they tucked her in, hugged her and said good-bye.

Meg shut her eyes quickly. She wasn't sure if she could bear to watch her parents walk out of the room, her father standing back politely, letting her mother go first.

Then Grandma brought the hot water bottle, in case her feet were cold. They were. Really, she felt cold all over, but she wasn't sure if it had anything to do with the temperature of her body. It was a sad cold, a desolate cold. And it went deep inside. Right into her bones.

She reached for Jessie, not even glancing at the still, bland face.

Grandma stayed with her, straightening the curtains, stacking the books on the bedside table, while the footsteps went down the stairs, the front door shut softly behind them, and the car doors slammed. Then the motor started and they were gone.

Meg wished Grandma would go away so that she could cry. She turned closer to Jessie and pretended to go to sleep. She would cry as soon as Grandma left.

She felt like she was being shaken, heard a terrible screeching noise and wakened on the pile of quilts. The wagon was moving. She sat up.

Meg could see the mother sitting on the seat on the front of the wagon, her arm around Lizzie. Archy was sitting beside her, driving the oxen. Meg could see them straining to pull the wagon as it lurched over the uneven ground.

"Gee! Gee!" he was yelling.

The screeching noise was coming from somewhere ahead of them. She couldn't see very well with all the boxes and bags stacked around her. She could hear the chickens, so their crates must be in there somewhere too.

"Do you want to come up and sit on the seat awhile, Morag?"

Meg climbed up beside them. The seat was high and supported by strips of metal that gave, like springs, so it wasn't quite as rough as riding down in the wagon. She held on as tightly as she could. It seemed that the broad backs of the oxen were right below her. She was up high enough to see right over the wagon load now and could see that the screeching noise was coming from the cart the man called Papa was driving. It was the one he'd been fixing, with large wooden wheels, pulled by a tough-looking white pony with a black mane and tail and black rings around the eyes. She hadn't seen it before. Nor had she seen all the cattle that were coming out of the trees behind them.

"As soon as we get to that rise, Papa said we're to stop and wait to make sure Geordie's got the cattle all rounded up. Morag can help him, now she's had her rest." The boy Archy was looking at her with a warm grin. "She's the best one with those cows."

I am? thought Meg. But strangely enough she wasn't afraid and when she ran back a few minutes later she seemed to know what to do all right. Jerk Geordie was glad to see her too.

"Evangeline is missing but the herd'll follow the lead cow now she's started after the wagon. Come and help me look. I'm afraid she's dropped her calf. She's gone into

28

hiding anyway." He started back into the clump of poplar. "Cooo boss! Cooo boss!"

Meg followed, moving a little over into a hollow that might hold a cow. She wasn't sure she wanted to find this Evangeline anyway. And what did he mean, 'dropping her calf'? As if cows carried them around like babies in their arms—legs.

She was relieved to see there was no cow ahead of her. Then she heard Geordie's voice. "Morag, come quick, I've found her!"

Just then he burst out of the bush pursued by a red cow. A very large, red cow it seemed to Meg. She jumped behind a tree but the cow stopped short and turned and ran back into the bushes.

Geordie came over. "She's calved all right. She's just protecting her calf. Never did like me. She likes you though, 'cause you always used to sneak out to the barn and feed her potatoes. You'll have to go in there and get her so I can carry the calf up to ride in the cart with Papa. It's too little to follow the herd."

Meg was astounded. She searched this boy's face for signs that he just had a warped sense of humour, but he looked serious all right. He actually thought that she would go in that bush with a mad cow!

"She's got a rope on her neck. Once you've got her calmed down, you can lead her with that while I carry the calf. Papa will be so pleased that he didn't have to stop and come back to help us. I can just see Mother's face when she sees that calf. It's a beauty!"

Meg inched toward the bush the cow had gone into.

"Hurry, Morag! We'll be a long way behind if they started again when they saw the herd coming. I'd better stay back here until you call me."

Meg turned to glare at him but he looked so eager she realized he really thought she could tame this beast.

She pushed through the bushes. There they were. The

tiny red and white calf lying curled up just like Bambi, the mother licking it and making low mooing sounds.

Meg walked closer. I don't believe this. I've never been this close to a cow since I was a kid and we went to the petting zoo. And here I am acting like a lion tamer . . . a cow tamer at least.

"Nice cow . . . nice Evangeline!"

"Moo," said Evangeline. It was not exactly an unfriendly tone of voice, but decidedly less friendly than the one she was using to her baby.

Meg stopped. "Nice Evangeline . . . nice cow . . ." How do you talk to a cow? she wondered. She remembered Geordie. "Cooo boss . . ." she said softly.

Evangeline just kept licking. Meg decided that she would approach from the side; that way Evangeline wouldn't think she was going to harm the calf. "Cooo boss . . . nice Evangeline . . ." She was really quite close now and so far the cow hadn't moved.

I wonder if a cow gives any kind of signal, like switching its tail or something, before it attacks? Oh well, Meg thought, I expect I'll wake up if anything like that happens; you do in dreams. She reached out and touched the shoulder of the cow.

Nothing happened.

Evangeline just kept licking her calf. Meg stroked the sleek shoulder, working her way up the bumpy neck towards the rope. Evangeline swung her head towards Meg and licked her arm! Even through her flannel sleeve Meg could feel how rough the cow's tongue was. Like Possum's tongue but, of course, much bigger.

She looked up to see Geordie had moved into sight and was watching from the bushes. He spoke softly, excitedly.

"You've done it, Morag! You really have a way with that cow!" He edged forward towards the calf. "Cooo boss, cooo boss."

Evangeline mooed a warning. There was no doubt in Meg's mind that's what it was, deep and threatening, not like the soft moos for the calf and her or the loud calling moos she had heard from the other cows when she'd passed the herd. Good grief, she thought, I'm beginning to understand Cow!

Geordie had stopped at the warning. "She doesn't want me near the calf. See if she'll let you touch it."

Meg kept her hand at the cow's head so that when Evangeline bent to lick, Meg's hand was a little behind. The calf was wet from being born and all that licking, but it was lovely and soft. She stroked the little head and kept on petting it even after Evangeline raised her head. Evangeline not only did not seem to mind, she mooed her loving moo and licked Meg right across the forehead.

"Ouch!" Meg started to giggle.

Geordie looked discouraged. "It's not funny. Now we'll have to get Papa or Archy. That calf's too heavy for you to carry."

Meg looked at the little thing. Compared to Evangeline it was awfully small. She bent down and tried to hold it the way she would Possum but it was too big and a lot heavier than she'd thought.

"I've got an idea, Morag! Maybe if you come over and take me by the hand and lead me to Evangeline, she'll let me come up to the calf. Just keep between me and her."

"Oh great, then she'll trample me to get at you!" But Meg moved away from the calf towards Geordie.

As they started back, Evangeline mooed again. This time though Meg thought it sounded more questioning than threatening.

"It's all right, Evangeline . . . good cow . . . nice cow . . . cooo boss," she said softly as she brought Geordie around beside the cow, away from the calf.

They both petted Evangeline before kneeling down to pet the calf, always talking softly.

"Now," said Geordie, quietly, "I'll pick the calf up, holding it between me and Evangeline, and if that works

31

you slip under her neck and hold the rope. Then if that works we'll start walking."

Very slowly, talking and petting, they did it. Now Meg was on one side of the cow holding the rope and Geordie on the other holding the calf close to its mother's head. The next part would be tricky, Meg thought. When Geordie starts walking with the calf Evangeline may think he's stealing her baby and if he thinks I can hold onto a charging cow, he's crazy!

"All right Morag, we'll start walking when I say three ... one, two ... three!"

Meg took a step forward, so did Geordie—so did Evangeline! Another step. They were doing it! True, Evangeline was not mooing her 'I love you' moo. More like an 'I'm not sure what's going on here ... don't hurt my baby' moo. But at least it wasn't an angry sound and she was walking quietly between Meg and the calf and Geordie. They came out of the bushes and started down the hillside.

They could see the last of the cows going over the top of the rise where Meg had left the wagon. There was Archy coming towards them.

They quickened their pace a little, not too much so as not to upset Evangeline, but she didn't seem to mind and seemed to be moving faster herself, now she had seen the herd. It was as if she understood what they were trying to do.

Archy met them and carefully changed places with his brother. Geordie's arms must have been getting awfully tired, Meg thought, but he was not complaining, just telling Archy how bravely Meg had tamed the cow after it had charged him.

"What is it?" Archy asked.

Meg almost said, "It's a calf, stupid," but Geordie answered, "A heifer! Won't Mother be pleased! She was so disappointed when the last two were bull calves."

I guess that means it's a girl, thought Meg.

With Archy carrying the calf and Evangeline walking fast to catch up with the herd, Meg was almost having to run to keep up. Soon they were on top of the hill and could see the pony and cart stopped on top of the next one with the wagon almost caught up to it. The cows straggled behind in the valley.

Meg remembered something. "Who's driving the oxen?"

Archy laughed. "Mother, of course. You aren't the only Shearer woman who knows how to handle animals! Geordie, run ahead and tell Papa to wait with the cart so the calf can ride."

Geordie ran and before they loaded the calf into the cart, Archy set it down on its wobbly legs beside Evangeline. It butted the udder with its little head and had a drink of milk as if it had been doing it all its life.

Meg lay in the quilts holding Jessie that night, feeling happy inside. At supper (the rabbit stew tasted pretty good after all, like chicken, sort of) everyone made a big fuss over her. And she had decided Geordie wasn't such a jerk after all. He'd told the truth about who it was had got the calf first . . . well, perhaps he had exaggerated a little as to how far and fast the cow had chased *him!* But that just made 'our Morag' a bigger heroine to everyone.

Not only that, but when Papa had said Geordie should be the one to name the calf since he'd been the first to find it (that seemed to be the family rule), he'd said that it was really Morag should name it. So now she was going to be able to name Evangeline's baby girl . . . no, heifer calf. Except she was too tired to think of anything tonight; she'd do it in the morning.

5

She woke up feeling good, lying there with her eyes shut, savouring the feeling, expecting the smell of wood smoke. Wondering what to name the calf. Slowly she realized that she was back in the soft bed at Grandma's. Disappointed, she opened her eyes and found herself staring into Jessie's china-blue eyes.

Those eyes seemed different each time she looked at them. And yet they were just painted. Just blank blue painted eyes. But right now, for instance, they seemed to smirk at her. No, that's wrong, eyes don't smirk, she thought, but they did look triumphant. Smug. It made Meg nervous.

"Good morning, sleepyhead." Grandma was smiling at her from the doorway. "Nobody could complain that you're not getting enough sleep! Will you come down for breakfast again this morning?"

Then she remembered yesterday. Her mother and father had been here. And the sadness came back suddenly, washing over her like a wave. Drowning her.

"I don't . . ." Meg began, but her throat was tight and the words wouldn't come out. She sank back on the pillow.

Grandma didn't seem to notice. She turned back to the

door and seemed to be talking to someone. Then she came in carrying Old Poss and scolding him.

"There you are sitting out on the landing again . . . Silly Old Possum! Meg comes for a visit and you won't even come in and see her . . . I don't know what's come over you!"

Meg held out her arms to the cat, but its feet barely hit the covers before it was backing away from her. Hissing. Back arched, fur standing on end; Meg had never seen Possum's eyes look like this before. Hot yellow— almost shooting sparks.

". . . But Meg. He *likes* you! Possum Cat, what's got into you?"

Meg slipped quickly out of bed and moved around beside Grandma. Possum didn't move. Tail straight up on end and twice its normal size, he pressed against the board at the foot of the bed. His hissing changed to a deep growl directed at the head of the bed where Meg had been.

"It's not me he's growling at," Meg said pointing at the doll, "It's Jessie!"

Grandma sounded relieved. "Well of all the silly cats!"

She reached over and picked up the doll, bringing it closer to the snarling cat. Possum flashed off the bed and out the door. Meg heard the thump of his feet as he raced down the stairs.

"Isn't that the strangest thing? It's the doll all right." Grandma stared at the china face.

Meg knew it was true. It was as if Poss knew something about the doll. Something Meg wasn't sure she wanted to know herself. She turned towards the door. Grandma was looking around the room, shaking her head. "It's the strangest thing. And you know what else? It smells peculiar in here!"

Meg knew what it was. There was the smell of cow all over her hands. She turned towards the door. "I'll just wash and be down for breakfast. Right away."

She stood before the bathroom sink, staring at her face in the mirror as if she'd never seen it before.

What if it wasn't a dream!

What if she was stiff and sore not just from rheumatic fever but because yesterday she'd really been out on the prairie—sleeping on the ground, following a Red River cart?

She really had felt the itch of the stockings ... the roughness of Evangeline's tongue. Meg stared at her hands. The cold water running over them should have been a shock but she hardly felt it. She remembered how often since she'd been sick she'd felt this way. As if she wasn't really part of things, as though it was happening to someone else. As if *now* was the dream.

"Breakfast's ready, Meg!" Grandma's voice came from the kitchen.

Meg stared at herself in the mirror. The short, brown hair, like a tousled cap on her head framed a still, pale face. Only the frightened eyes gave life to it. It seemed to move, to fade in and out. Dreamlike. For a moment, she could see it reflected in the water—the same face but with the hair ending in long, thick braids. Then it seemed to ripple and change back.

She had to fight to speak. "I'm coming Grandma." Her voice sounded strange too as if now was the dream.

She really had been a girl called Morag.

What if Meg was only part of a dream? A dream Morag was dreaming. . . . The thought was too big to hold in her mind. She couldn't bear it.

Her knees felt weak and she grabbed the sink for support.

"Meg! Are you coming down?"

She walked out of the bathroom, feeling weak. As if she wasn't really doing the walking. As if somehow, she was a puppet.

As she crossed the landing she looked through the open door. Lying propped up against the pillows the doll's eyes seemed to bore into her. No, not into her . . . through her. She was grateful that her feet seemed to move her automatically down the hall; otherwise she could not have looked away from those staring eyes.

The bannister was smooth, worn, and somehow comforting against the palm of her hand and she clung to it for support. She was relieved at last to be sitting at the kitchen table.

"Are you still tired, Meg?" There was Grandma's hand on her forehead again, like a caress. "You seemed to be sleeping like a log every time I looked in on you."

Meg didn't say anything. What could she say?

"Your dad phoned . . . to see how you were . . . but he said he'd call you later." Grandma Grace hesitated. I can't very well tell her he's phoned to give me his new phone number, she thought, and to tell me to call if there's anything we need. "He loves you, Meg," was all she could think of to say.

Before yesterday Meg would have thought that a strange thing to say. Of course she knew it was true . . . but now there were doubts. About other things. Where did she fit in her parents' world now? She nodded silently.

She watched Possum rubbing up against Grandma's leg as she brought Meg her plate of scrambled eggs.

"How many eggs in that, Grandma?"

Grandma looked surprised. "Three, but you don't have to eat it all, dear."

Meg thought of her other family and how happy they'd be to have all these eggs. There'd be one for each of them counting the five she and Geordie had gathered, with an extra one each for Mother and Papa. She realized that she didn't feel very hungry and that it seemed as though she'd just eaten something. Of course . . . rabbit stew! It had been so nice sitting around the campfire, everyone so pleased about the calf . . . her calf.

"Grandma," she said, reaching down to pat Possum

who was rubbing against her leg purring his wheezy, old-cat purr, "What's a good name for a heifer calf?"

Grandma looked at her strangely and Meg realized that her questions didn't follow, or make much sense. "I . . . I mean, what did you name your cows when you were a little girl on the farm?"

Grandma smiled. "My goodness, Meg, I haven't thought about that in years." She stopped eating her oatmeal and sat with a remembering smile on her face. "We seemed to always have the same names over and over. We just kept using the names my great-grandparents had for their herd when they first came west. There was always an Adeline, a Clementine, and what was the other? Oh yes, an Evangeline! Of course, we had pedigreed cattle by then and so their names were longer, but we always had those names in somewhere. I remember Clementine was a miserable beast, always trying to kick me when it was my turn to do the milking. Is that all you're going to eat, dear?"

Meg felt she couldn't force another forkful into her mouth. She was grateful that just then there was a knock on the back door and the cheerful face of Mrs. Schaefer, Grandma's next door neighbour, poked in.

"Good thing the coffee's still fresh, Berta!" Grandma was already pouring a cup as her friend tossed a bundle of letters and magazines onto the table. "You're early today!"

Berta Schaefer was already making herself comfortable. "I always like to get to the post office while they're still sorting. That way Maisie doesn't get a chance to read my postcards!" She dumped several teaspoons of sugar into her coffee. "And how's the patient today?"

"Fine," said Meg. She was watching Grandma sort out the bills, the local paper, and a couple of gardening magazines. There looked to be only one real letter. To her surprise Grandma handed it to her.

"Vancouver, Meg? You've got a pen pal?"

Meg didn't even have to look at the envelope to know

it was from Allison. Good old Allison! Meg had written from the hospital as soon as she knew she was coming to Grandma's. She hadn't expected a reply this fast. Allison was not the world's greatest letter writer; usually she only wrote once for every two letters Meg wrote. And then her letters were mostly cartoons. She wished Allison would write longer letters. She always read them over and over and felt cheered up afterwards.

"It's from Allison. Remember? She came with me to visit you last summer. Her parents broke up just after that and she had to move to Vancouver with her mum." Meg wasn't sure why she added that. It wasn't just to see the expression change on Grandma's face. It was because she felt if she said it, the idea would seem natural and be easier to get used to.

She picked up the letter. As usual the envelope was scribbled over with Allison-type remarks. Arrows at one end: To Open Chew Here, and all across the back: This Envelope is Security Protected! (Stomper Wombat Security Systems). There were several drawings of small animals looking fierce and shaking their fists. Meg couldn't help laughing.

She excused herself. "I'll just go up to my room for a while. Is there some writing paper? I can answer the letter."

Grandma handed her a writing pad and pen from the top of the fridge and then settled back down with her coffee. "Run along then. I'll bring you an envelope and stamp later."

Running was the last thing Meg could do. She stopped beside Possum who was now curled up in a patch of sunlight on the floor. "Coming Poss?" But he only opened one eye, looked at her, and closed it again. She remembered her dad saying Possum was the only cat he'd ever met who wore a Do Not Disturb sign.

She could hear Mrs. Schaefer's voice from the kitchen. "Such a quiet, well-behaved girl, Grace!"

It made Meg want to stomp up the stairs, whoop a little

and perhaps break something for good measure, but she just smiled, enjoying the thought of Mrs. Schaefer's reaction. She'd learned that imagining doing crazy things was almost as much fun as doing them and got her into a lot less trouble.

She climbed the stairs slowly, reading more of Allison's envelope. One of the wombats was carrying a sign: Wombat Power. She ripped open the envelope where it said Open Other End and curled up on the bed to read.

The letter was pure Allison. Not much writing, lots of cartoons. Went to Aquarium on Field Trip was the heading over a troop of stick children walking by tanks of fish. Several octopus arms were protruding from a huge tank and grabbing a large stick person labelled: Miss Winthrop. A person obviously swimming in a pool followed by a shark fin was labelled: Me! with the words 'Had an interesting day' written underneath. The last picture was a school bus driving away with heads, legs, and arms (some of which waved fish) poking out of the windows. It was pursued by a large octopus wearing a ladies' hat and carrying a purse. So educational! was the caption. Meg chuckled. Good old Allison. She'd managed to cover a whole page without even one sentence. She looked at the second page. No pictures! Allison had actually written something!

Dear Meg,
You asked how I managed to survive the move to Vancouver. Leaving my dad and all that. Well, to tell the truth, being this far away beats the back and forth weekend stuff. I know that sounds awful. And I do miss him. But it really was a pain. I felt like the rope in a tug-of-war. Remember how I bragged about all the presents I was getting when they first split? Well, it wasn't long before I found out it wasn't that great. I mean, it was no fun getting something from Dad that I really loved and

40

then going back to Mum's and having her sort of mad and resentful because she couldn't afford to buy it for me. So then I'd have to pretend I didn't really like the present after all. That's why moving was a blessing in a way. The new school wasn't great at first, but lots of other kids were new too, so I managed okay. Really the only thing I miss about being away from Saskatoon is you, kiddo! And here's the GOOD NEWS!

The writing broke off again for arrows pointing to the next page. There was a picture of a parade. A highly decorated float holding a reclining figure in elegant clothes and sparkling jewels was being carried by several elephants or possibly, Meg thought, horses with trunks. The banner being carried said: Allison Returns. Crowds of stick people, their mouths round circles, obviously cheering, waved flags and threw what looked like money.

There was just one more sentence on the page. "I'm coming to visit my dad for part of the holidays—see you then!!!" The letter was signed, "your old friend, Allison" with 'old' underlined and one last picture: a wrinkly faced woman leaning on a cane with a very long beard. Meg leaned back smiling. Good old Allison.

She picked up the writing pad and started to draw. A boy being chased by a cow, herself like a matador waving a cape, a baby calf riding in a Red River cart. They weren't like Allison's drawings at all. They weren't great but they weren't cartoons either. They were serious. And real. Meg carefully tore the paper into tiny bits and dropped them into the wastebasket.

Grandma came in with an envelope just as Meg was climbing back into bed. "Here you are. Did you finish writing to Allison?"

"I decided not to . . . not much to tell her . . ." And if I did, she'd never believe it, Meg thought.

She lay very still as Grandma left. The bed was soft and

she was so tired. She closed her eyes. She had avoided looking at Jessie ever since she came in but she knew the doll was there, could feel her, lying on the covers almost touching Meg's arm. And she knew what she would do next, did it before she even thought about it. Automatically.

She reached for the doll, eyes closed, avoiding the stare of the china eyes. I think I'll just go name that calf.

She was not a bit surprised this time when she woke up on the ground between the quilts. It seemed to be very early in the morning, but Mother was up bustling about with a huge iron pot on the campfire. It reminded Meg of a witch's cauldron or one of those pots cartoon cannibals use to cook people. She hoped that it wasn't full of oatmeal porridge.

She sat up and realized that the other children were still sleeping. There was Lizzie lying next to Meg with her arm thrown casually across Jessie.

"Oh Morag, I'm glad you've wakened. I thought I'd do a washing before we set out. Let me have your stockings and petticoat; there's fresh ones on the foot of the quilt. It looks to be a nice day coming and we can dry things as we go along."

Meg was relieved to slip the stockings off. But when she put the fresh pair on they were just as bad, just as itchy as the others had been.

Mother watched her with a little smile. "It will be nice when we get to the homestead and can sleep in nightdresses again instead of going to sleep with half our clothes on." She gave Meg a hug. It was a happy hug. Meg decided it was going to be a good day, itchy stockings or not.

She watched as Mother put the underclothes into the cauldron of hot, soapy water and stirred it with a stick just as if she were making soup. Petticoat soup. Meg almost giggled. And stockings and meatballs, she thought, picturing it. Mother lifted the steaming clothes out with the stick and dropped them with a splosh into another pan. Then she put the boys' shirts into the water.

"You stir these for a bit, Morag, while I rinse the others."

Meg took the stick and began to stir. I'm making shirt soufflé, she thought.

Mother's hands looked awfully red as she wrung out Meg's clothes and then plunged them into a smaller pot of water, rinsing them around and then wringing them out and putting them in a large basket with a pile of other clothes. She looked over at Meg.

"That's enough, you can lift them out for me now."

Meg thought she sploshed the shirts into the pan like an expert. She bent over to pick one up to wring it out but it was awfully hot and she dropped it quickly.

"Oooh Morag, don't lass, you'll burn your hands. Besides, those shirts are too big for you to wring." Mother held one up to drip. "They hold the heat. Even I have to let them cool a wee bit and my hands are tough." They looked sore to Meg but she didn't say anything. "You can help by waking Lizzie and the others."

Meg went over. She noticed Archy was already up; he seemed to be cutting some long poles. She stood looking down at Geordie. If he hadn't been so nice yesterday she would have taken great pleasure in thinking up a particularly nasty kind of awakening for him. As it was she was very tempted. Her hesitation saved him. He opened his eyes and saw her staring at him.

"Morag! *You* up before me! The age of miracles hasn't passed, as Granny Shearer would say!" He was up and pulling on the faded black pants that were just a smaller version of Papa's.

Lizzie woke up immediately. "Mooog! . . ." She sat for a minute smiling sleepily at Meg. Then her face brightened, she saw Mother and the cauldron, and was up and away. Meg caught her.

"Whoa . . . let me put your dress on. It's too chilly to

run around in your . . . your petticoat." She dressed Lizzie and gave her a little hug. She felt like it.

She decided she would help out by folding up the quilts. They were thick and heavy and she had to flop back and forth with them, but at last they were folded in a pile although not as neatly as Mother had done it. She was just trying to figure out how she would get them into the wagon when Archy came by and scooped up an armful and did it for her.

"You should see that calf of yours this morning, Morag. She's a strong one. I'll finish this. You go take a look at her before we eat."

Meg followed the sound of the cattle. There were Evangeline and the calf, steady on its feet now, exploring the world with its nose. Evangeline mooed and Meg squatted near her so as not to frighten the baby. The little thing seemed to be trying to eat grass but it was just sniffing. Then Meg saw it was sniffing a little yellow flower.

"Well, what are you going to name her?" Geordie had come up so quietly Meg nearly fell over.

"Ummmm . . . I think I'll call her Buttercup," Meg said.

"That's a new one. Time we got away from all the Adelines and Evangelines." He tweaked her braid. Hard enough that Meg decided that next time she had a chance to wake him, the truce was over. "Come on, sister dear, it's time for prayers. And . . . there's eggs for breakfast!"

Meg almost groaned aloud. She was going to have to eat again!

It turned out that they were one egg short and Mother was going to go without. Everybody wanted to give her their egg.

"But I'd really rather just have oatmeal," Meg argued. I hope there's a rosebush handy, she thought.

She helped load the chicken crates into the wagon. I'm working harder than I've ever worked at home. Of course she had her room to clean and she always got her own lunch because her mother was at work, but those were things she did for herself. Now she was working for everybody. They all were . . . like a team.

She could see Archy attaching the poles he had cut to the sides of the wagon box so that they stood straight up. At first she couldn't imagine what they were for. But when she saw him tying a cord across between them she guessed. A clothesline! The wash would flap in the breeze and dry as the wagon rolled along!

"Morag, would you sit with Lizzie on the wagon seat? Archy can't.hold her and drive too."

That was fine with Meg. She liked sitting up on the wagon seat with Lizzie in the middle so she wouldn't fall. The sun was warm and with the clothes like banners fluttering from the wagon, she felt like the lead float in a parade. A mighty strange parade, with the pony and cart creaking along behind and the cows straggling out like a fan behind them. Still, Meg felt important, as if she should be waving to the crowds.

Instead, she waved to a couple of gophers standing at attention like an honour guard on the hillside.

6

Meg hadn't realized it before but they were following a trail. Deep ruts cut through the grass. "It's almost a road!" she said, surprised.

Archy laughed. "Not really, but it's been used a lot by people like us. It's called the Carlton Trail and that's as far as we go . . . to Fort Carlton."

Meg wondered why that place sounded familiar. Then she remembered. Carlton was the place where Grandma had grown up.

"So we're getting close? I'm so glad . . . Mother is looking forward to the house."

Archy laughed. "That will take more time than just getting there. There's logs to cut to build the house and we must put up some hay to get the stock through the winter. There may not be enough foraging for them in the bush." His expression turned more serious. "We'll manage fine . . . if the weather holds."

Meg almost blurted, "There's no house where we're going?" but then she thought about it. Of course there wouldn't be a house on a homestead. Not until somebody built one. Poor Mother, it would be a while before she got to sleep in a bed, in a nightdress, after all.

As they topped the next rise the landscape seemed to

change. Ahead there was a small lake, with cattails and reeds all around it. The tracks cut off sharply, skirting around the slough until they disappeared in a dip up ahead.

"Whoa!" Archy stopped the oxen and turned to Meg. "Run back to Papa and tell him we're getting close to the south branch."

Meg put her foot on the big wheel to climb down but just then the wagon moved. Archy grabbed her just in time and pulled her back. She looked at him surprised and was even more surprised to see the worried look on his face.

"Morag! Don't ever climb down on the wheel when the critters are hitched up! If they move, your foot could be caught in the spokes. Don't you remember what happened to the girl back in Peterborough County? . . . broken leg and lucky to be alive after the wheel passed over her!"

Meg was shaken. She could imagine everything he was telling her . . . vividly. See herself dragged along. "I . . . I'm sorry . . ."

His grip on her arm loosened and he grinned. "Use the step. That's why Papa put it on."

She looked down at the side of the wagon box. There were two small wooden steps like a ladder nailed onto the box. She climbed down carefully, stepping out from between the wheels as quickly as she could.

"Lizzie come too!" She was bouncing up and down on the wagon seat. Archy lifted her across to Meg. Meg took her hand and started down the hill.

She could see the pony and cart and beyond it the straggling cattle with Geordie following. There was Buttercup following so close to Evangeline it was a wonder the little thing wasn't stepped on. The calf was a mixture of red and white all blended in together that Geordie called roan. It reminded Meg of the way strawberry jello looked when you beat it up with whipped cream.

Mother was sitting beside Papa while he drove the cart.

Meg thought they looked very nice together—in their old-fashioned way. She wondered if they had ever thought about breaking up. It seemed impossible. Unthinkable. But then, last year she would never have believed it could happen to her mum and dad either.

Lizzie tugged at Meg's hand, trying to run as they neared the cart. The parents waved. Meg thought how very special they were, building a life for their family out of practically nothing—just what they would find on their land. Carrying their whole world with them almost.

"Papa!" she called as they neared the cart. It surprised her. It was the first time she'd called him that except in her head, but it had popped out easily . . . naturally.

"We've made good time, if we're there already," he said when she told him her news. "Now we'll see if we can get through without getting stuck. Tell Geordie to let the cattle pasture here and come ahead and help."

Mother climbed off the cart and took Lizzie's hand, "And we'll help Morag keep herd so the cattle don't stray."

So now Meg sat on the hillside with Mother not far from her and Lizzie scampering here and there picking brown-eyed-susans so Mother could make crowns. She wasn't sure if it was the smell of the soft thin-leafed grass that nestled everywhere or the warm sun, but she was having a hard time keeping awake. She would just lie down for a minute but she wouldn't close her eyes, of course.

She was losing the battle to keep them open when she saw the animal. It was bigger than Old Poss, a lot bigger, heavier anyway, and it was running in a strange slouching way down the hillside toward Lizzie.

Maybe it didn't see the child but Meg wasn't taking any chances. She sprang up and yelled, "Lizzie!"

Now she was sure the animal had not seen any of them for, as she jumped up, it turned its strange flat-looking striped head toward her and headed back up the hill.

Lizzie only looked at Meg for a moment and then ran

after the animal, screeching with delight, "Wait! Wait for Lizzie!"

Mother was on her feet, scattering flowers in all directions, but Meg was closer, already running.

The animal moved quickly despite its awkward, ambling gait. It disappeared behind a bleached white boulder part way up the hill. Lizzie's short legs churned through the grass and flowers after it.

Meg was gaining on her when Lizzie disappeared behind the rock.

"Lizzie!" Meg called. She knew Mother was running but she was too far away.

It was up to Meg to do something. Fast. She dashed around the rock, not even daring to imagine what she might see.

What she saw was dirt. A storm of it flying from a large burrow. Clumps, bits, but mostly a cloud of dust and, in the midst of it, Lizzie part way into the hole holding onto something bushy.

"Lizzie! Let go!" Meg grabbed the child but she was afraid to pull. What if she pulled too hard and the animal turned around and attacked? Right now it seemed only interested in escape. Lizzie was hanging on with fierce determination and Meg could feel her being dragged into the burrow.

Meg hung on. "Motherrr!" she yelled. "Lizzie's got this thing by the tail!"

Mother was there, reaching around Meg to Lizzie and there was no mistaking her tone of voice. "Lizzie Ann Shearer, let go this minute!"

Lizzie lost her grip and they fell back in a heap in the dirt.

". . . She just kept hanging on, Mother . . . I couldn't get her to let go!"

"If that badger had turned around, he could have killed you! Lizzie, you can't pat every animal you see in the West."

They were drowned out by Lizzie's howls. "It got away . . . you made it get away!"

Meg sat there for a minute getting her breath. Her mouth was full of grit and she was sure her face was dirty. If it was half as black as Lizzie's it was bad, all right. Just now all that distinguished Lizzie from the famous Tar Baby was the wide open howling mouth. It wasn't helped by the two muddy rivulets of tears she had going. Meg looked at Mother sitting in the dirt scolding Lizzie.

". . . You're just a very lucky wee lass that Morag saw that beast and came after you . . ."

The dirt on Mother's face, especially around the eyes, gave her the look of a very angry raccoon. Meg started to giggle.

Mother stopped short, looked at Meg, and a slow crinkly smile began to grow into a laugh that bubbled up through the grime. Soon they were leaning against each other laughing while Lizzie, cut off in midhowl, looked at them with shock.

That was how Geordie found them when he came with the news that the wagon was stuck and they would have to camp there for the night while Archy and Papa used the daylight hours to unload and move everything across the slough.

Geordie was impressed by their adventure. "A badger! But they can beat a dog if they're cornered!"

"This one was cornered all right." Mother was emphatic. "I think he was just digging that burrow and hadn't made it wide enough to turn around in. If he had, the Dear knows what would have happened!"

"Oh, Morag would have wrestled him to a standstill . . . she's tough." Geordie looked at her. "Tough and dirty . . . that is!"

Meg ignored him. One of these days she'd show Jerk Geordie how tough she was.

They had to tell their story again to Archy and Papa. By now Lizzie got in on the telling.

"Lizzie had a nice doggie . . ."

"I'm not sure who had who," Meg interrupted. "That badger was digging so fast and Lizzie was holding on so tight that I thought she would disappear down the hole just like Alice . . ."

"Alice?" said Archy. Everyone looked at Meg expectantly.

"You know, like Alice in Wonderland, down the rabbit hole," Meg explained. She watched their puzzled faces.

Oh no, she thought, they don't know what I'm talking about. Maybe *Alice in Wonderland* hasn't been written yet.

"It's just a story I heard . . . about a little girl and a rabbit hole," Meg explained lamely.

"Tell Lizzie a story . . . a rabbit story!"

"That would be nice, Morag. It's time for her to sleep. You could rest a wee while and tell the story."

It sounded like a good idea to Meg. She had almost fallen asleep on the hillside.

"Come on Lizzie, I'll tell you and Jessie Doll all about Alice's adventures down the rabbit hole."

It took her a little while to locate Jessie. She wasn't in the pile of quilts where Meg was sure she'd left her. But then everything had been moved from the wagon when it got stuck. Meg saw the doll lying in a rut where it had fallen during the unloading. Jessie was wet and muddy. Were the china eyes looking annoyed?

Meg didn't care. Mother took the dress off to wash and carefully wiped the china head clean. The body was another matter but they squeezed it out and wrapped it in a towel.

"Story, Moog. Rabbit!" Lizzie was waiting, lying on the pile of quilts, patting the pillow beside her.

This is going to be a short one, thought Meg, lying down gratefully.

"Once upon a time, there was a little girl named Alice," Meg began. But she didn't get very far, not much beyond the drowsy day and Alice sitting beside her sister on the bank. Meg found that part very easy to describe. She felt a bit like Alice herself. Alice Through the Looking Glass.

She and Lizzie were curled up on the hillside beside the slough, the sun was pleasant, and the wind that whispered secrets to the long prairie grass beyond them was soft and soothing. She could not have told which of them fell asleep first.

7

Meg's grandmother stood beside the bed watching her. It was good to see Meg sleeping so well. Getting lots of rest. Getting better. So why, Grace Cameron asked herself, did she feel so uneasy? She didn't usually watch Meg sleep. Just looked in the door from time to time to make sure she was all right. But watching now, steadily for a long time, it seemed that Meg was strangely still. Surely she should be moving about a little? The girl lay there, her face pale and fixed. Unnaturally still—like a statue. Like the doll lying beside her.

Poor Meg. Perhaps Mark and Janet should have told her about the divorce. Now that there seemed to be no chance of them patching things up there wasn't much use in pretending. If she was any judge of expression, Meg knew anyway. Knew even the day she'd arrived. Maybe they were being unfair not to talk about it openly. By protecting Meg they were isolating her. Keeping her out of the family problems more than her sickness and being away from home had done.

Perhaps she should talk to Mark and Janet, try to persuade them. She reminded herself that grandparents often have as little control over the way parents decide things for a child as the child does. To tell the truth, this time she wasn't sure if there was a better way to handle the situation.

She remembered the night they'd come to tell Meg. It just hadn't seemed the right time. Meg had seemed so ill, so defenceless, that to add this burden would have been too much.

She wandered about the room, straightening chairs noisily, closing the old wooden-sashed window with a bang. She hoped Meg would wake up.

Her hands moved automatically, straightening the brush and comb on the dresser, stacking the books on the night table. Meg seemed happy enough here. Of course she had always been a quiet child, not one to complain or express her feelings much. Since the illness she seemed somehow preoccupied . . . withdrawn. What was it the doctor had said? Aside from the physical symptoms after rheumatic fever, being tired and stiff . . . something about being vague . . . daydreaming? He called it a 'fugue state' or something. He said she needed lots of rest and she was certainly getting that.

She started to leave the room, and saw the cat in the hall outside. Old Possum sat, motionless, staring into the room. His eyes seemed to glow as he glared at the bed.

Grace Cameron hesitated and turned back to her granddaughter. Wonderful how fond Meg had become of that old doll. The Invalid Doll. She stared at the stark china face. She wanted Meg awake. Now.

"Meg! Meg! Wake up!" There was no response.

She resisted the impulse to shake Meg. Outside the door Possum hissed, startling her so that she jumped slightly and turned towards him. She gazed into the golden eyes for a moment, then turning back to the bed, seized the doll and held it firmly at arms length, staring at it.

Meg opened her eyes. It seemed to her as if she'd just closed them on the drowsy hillside.

"Do you want to come down for supper?"

Meg started to sit up. Her body felt so heavy. And tired—very, very tired.

"Ooooh," she groaned. It wasn't exactly ouch but it was in the same spirit.

Grandma looked concerned. "What's wrong dear?"

Meg realized her mistake right away and sat up. "Just a little stiff, I guess."

Grandma piled up the pillows. "Perhaps you should stay in bed. Why don't you just look at one of your books and I'll bring you a sandwich and a glass of milk."

She lay the doll down and began straightening blankets. "Guess what? Your dad phoned. He's coming out tonight. I think he has a surprise for you!"

"A surprise?" Possibilities raced through Meg's mind, none of them pleasant. A present before he tells me he's moved out? she wondered. "Is it . . . a good surprise?" she asked hesitantly. Her eyes filled with tears and she turned her head quickly, angry with herself, hoping Grandma hadn't noticed.

Grandma hadn't. She was straightening Meg's covers. She flipped the bedspread and sent Jessie tumbling over the side of the bed. Meg lunged to save her, but the doll seemed to move on her own, pausing at the edge of the bed and then toppling with a crash to the floor.

"Oh no!" The anguish in her voice surprised Meg.

"Dear, dear!" Grandma bent and picked up the doll. The china head was intact, the face unspoiled, although Meg thought the eyes had a malicious gleam.

"She's all right." Grandma sounded relieved. She checked the china arms and legs. "No broken bones, Jessie, old girl." She squeezed the stuffed body thoughtfully. "That's strange . . ." She held the doll to her nose for a moment, then stared, sniffed, and sniffed again. "Jessie doesn't smell of mothballs anymore! Musty! She smells musty." She stared at Meg with an expression of disbelief. "I know as well as you do that this doll hasn't

55

been anywhere but the cedar chest and your bed, but if I didn't know it for a fact, I'd swear it's been sleeping in a ditch!"

Grandma sat the doll firmly on the dresser. "I'll have to figure out a way to freshen Jessie up. But first things first. I'll fetch you a bite to eat, Meg."

Meg didn't want to stay in the room any longer. She threw back the covers.

"No . . . no . . . I'll come downstairs."

She crawled out of bed, put on her housecoat and walked to the bathroom. Moving reminded her of how stiff she was. As if her joints should be creaking like rusty hinges on a door. She felt, she decided, just like the tin woodman sounded whenever Dorothy forgot to use the oil can on him.

She started to giggle and then, catching a glimpse of her face in the bathroom mirror, she froze. The smile. The little crinkly smile. That's why it had seemed familiar. It was Mother's in the dream that was not a dream—and it was hers too.

Once again she was standing, staring in the mirror, wondering who she was. Who she really was. Alice Through the Looking Glass.

"Are you all right, Meg?" Grandma stood in the doorway. "Do you need help?"

"No . . . no . . . I'm okay." She followed Grandma downstairs, glad of the support of the bannister, walking her tin woodman walk. In the kitchen she curled up on the window seat and watched as Grandma fixed the sandwiches for their supper. Poss strolled regally into the kitchen, across the room, and jumped up on the seat beside her.

She stroked his bushy fur. "Who do I look like, Grandma?"

Grandma looked thoughtful. "I'm not sure, Meg dear. You've got the dark hair like the Thompson side but then we've had that shade of brown too. You don't look that much like either of your parents . . . I tell you what, why don't we look through the old family albums tomorrow and see."

Meg ate most of the sandwich and drank all the milk. She was just finishing when the doorbell rang and Grandma went to answer it.

A moment later her father's face peeked round the door. He was alone and she forgot her stiffness for a moment as she ran to meet him.

Mark Thompson hugged Meg for a long time. He realized it was probably too long, but he didn't want to let go. As if somehow he could let her know that what was happening to Janet and himself had nothing to do with Meg. He wished he could say something. Tell her. But even as the thought crossed his mind, he knew that although the reasons for the break-up had nothing to do with Meg, the results had everything to do with her. He knew it, and he suspected from the way his daughter clung to him, that she did too.

Then she looked up at him and he wondered if they would ever be able to get over this desperate holding on. I'm not leaving you, Meg, he wanted to shout, and yet he was. He had already moved out. And now that the fights were over at last and the decision made, the relief he felt was at times outweighed by the fear that things would never be quite the same with his daughter. Suppers together, when Janet had to work late; could they ever go back to the easy fun they'd had? And then, when the only thing he could think of was to hug Meg again, she gave him hope.

She blurted the first thing she could think of. "So! How's Rosie O'Malley these days?" Her voice cracked but at least she'd tried. It was his turn now.

He looked surprised, then smiled, his face relaxing. "Rosie . . . um . . . Oh yes, Rosie . . ."

"Remember? Rosie and the Tower of London?" she prompted.

He looked crestfallen. "Meg baby, I'm afraid I've got a confession to make . . . about Rosie . . ."

Something inside Meg's chest hurt. Were all the games over? Only serious, sad things between them from now on? Please, Daddy . . . she wanted to beg.

He looked serious. "You see, the tower Rosie was mixed up with? Well, it wasn't much of a tower . . . more like a phone booth!"

Meg started to feel much better.

". . . Oh, it was in London all right . . . London, Ontario. You see, Rosie used to stand beside this phone booth and fire the starting gun for a car race that went across country."

A smile, a crinkly smile was spreading over Meg's face. "Oh sure, I'll bet!" she said, teasing. Inside she was cheering.

"Sure thing!" He gave her his Scout's honour salute. "Why surely you've heard of the famous O'Malley Rally!"

This time it was a happy hug.

"The surprise is up in your room, Meg!" announced Grandma, coming into the kitchen.

"Pretty sneaky!" said Meg, crossing the kitchen as quickly as she could with her creaky legs. Poss thumped after her following her up the stairs to his place outside her door.

She opened the door.

It was Allison! Smiling. Sitting there, waiting politely.

"Allison!" There was no doubt that Meg was surprised . . . and delighted. But then she didn't know what to say. She climbed onto the bed and sat crosslegged facing her friend.

There was an awkward silence for a moment as they sat smiling at each other, waiting to see who'd speak first. Meg was afraid she'd say something stupid. She did.

"Your hair's longer!"

Allison giggled. So did Meg.

The giggles faded nervously. It had been nearly eight months since they'd seen each other. Meg thought Allison looked different. She could tell from the way Allison was looking at her that she was noticing how different Meg looked too. She tried again.

"I mean . . . it looks great . . . you look great! . . . I got your letter. How long are you staying with your dad? There isn't a chance you'll be staying to go to school?"

Wouldn't that be great, Meg thought. I could handle anything if Allison was back. She dreaded the thought of going back to school. She'd missed her friend so much.

Allison was still looking at her.

"Boy! You must have been sick! I didn't know you'd been *that* sick! I knew you were in hospital and had been out of school for a long time, but I didn't know you'd look so pale and skinny!" Allison's hand flew to her mouth. "Ooops! Sorry! Not very nice . . ." She looked concerned. "You *are* better now, aren't you?"

Meg nodded. The laughter welled up inside. Good old Allison. The barriers were down; they could talk now. And they did. Meg tried to bring her up-to-date about kids they'd known at school. Allison described her new school, the kids, the apartment. She was just here to spend part of the holidays with her father.

"If you're here for the summer, we can get together . . . once I'm back home . . ." The wave of worry swept over Meg again. Where would that be? Would she be living in an apartment somewhere with her mother? Or her father? Or somewhere between? Tugged back and forth between parents the way Allison had described? Maybe she should tell Allison about her parents. Maybe that would help.

"I've missed having you to talk to . . ." her voice trailed off. She couldn't do it. It would make it too real.

"Me too."

There was an uncomfortable silence.

Allison jumped up. "Where's the bathroom?"

"Across the hall."

"Be right back."

Meg had forgotten the way Allison bounced around, dashing everywhere. So much energy all the time. The way she did just now, springing up and out the door. She popped back in even faster than she had gone out and stood there looking at Meg with a peculiar expression on her face.

"Ummm . . . Meg . . . have you got a watch cat?"

Meg laughed. "A what?"

"There's an enormous fat cat sitting out there simply glaring. What's up? Is he jealous of you having a visitor?"

"No . . . not exactly. Not jealous of you anyway. He's really quite a friendly cat."

"He won't attack or anything?"

Meg couldn't believe it. Here was Allison. Dare-a-day-Allison. Allison, the sure-of-herself. Allison who could cope with anything. Worried about Old Possum? And herself . . . Meg. Meg the short. Meg the timid. Afraid to ask questions or make friends. Meg had tamed a cow—saved a child from a badger. Sort of. It was quite a switch.

"I'll go with you," she said smiling.

"Hey, I can handle it," said Allison in her old Allison way. "Wrestle my weight in wildcats . . . Well, your weight, anyway!" They both laughed.

But Meg noticed that Allison made sure she kept Meg between herself and Possum as she crossed to the bathroom.

Possum *was* looking large, larger than usual. The fur on his back stood on end as he stared through the open bedroom door at the doll on the dresser. A low growl vibrated in his throat.

Meg shut the door firmly. "Come on, Possum! Come sit with me on the stairs if you won't come in my room." The old cat came immediately and she smoothed the fierce fur. Soon his rumbling changed to the raggedy sort of purr that was the best he could do.

Allison came out and noticed them.

"What's this?" she laughed. "Where did the other cat

go?" She sat by Meg, tentatively reaching her hand out to pet the cat. Poss wheezed even louder and more enthusiastically. "What did you do? Hypnotize the animal?" Allison gazed into the yellow eyes. "Look into my eyes . . ."

The laughter faded on Meg's face and she looked at the closed bedroom door. She knew the doll's eyes were staring at her from within. She could feel them. She felt Poss stiffen and the purring stopped as if cut off somewhere in his throat.

"Meg! Meg! You okay?" Allison was watching her, sounding worried.

Meg could hear Dad and Grandma coming out of the kitchen, to the foot of the stairs.

"Did you two have a nice visit?" Her dad was smiling up at them. She thought he looked happier. Some of Grandma's nice hot cup of tea magic again? "I hate to break this up but I did promise Allison's dad I'd have her home early."

It wasn't so bad saying good-bye this time for either of them, but she was relieved when she finally got back into bed and Grandma kissed her good night.

"Jessie's going to get a bit of an airing before you sleep with her again, all right dear?"

Meg didn't really care. She was so tired and stiff. She lay there feeling warm and drowsy, almost asleep.

Just before she finally slept she was aware of something landing on the bed, moving beside her and then the sound of Old Poss's purring as he curled up close to her.

8

Grandma Grace finished rinsing the fragile old doll dress and laid it carefully on a towel to dry. She picked up the doll, sniffed it again, and shook her head.

"You smell a bit like a dog that's been swimming in the slough . . . How am I going to freshen you up, Jessie old doll?" She stared at the doll, nodded, and moved out of the kitchen.

Meg woke suddenly, eyes wide open in the dark. For a moment she wondered where she was, then, feeling the softness of the bed, she knew. She felt better—not so tired. She moved her legs—not so stiff. She flung her arm out to hold the doll and remembered Jessie was gone.

She felt incredibly lonely. As if she was the only person on some faraway planet. It was a terrible feeling.

She lay still, tense, eyes wide open, waiting for them to adjust to the black room. There was no streetlight to shine through the window the way it did in her room in the city. She could hardly tell where the window was. Gradually she got her bearings. She threw back the covers; at least she tried to. Something was holding them down. Something heavy. Meg froze. Slowly she began to wiggle out from under. The weight moved against her—and began to purr.

Meg could feel her stomach unclench, loosen, and relax. Poss! How could she have forgotten him? She patted him. "It's okay, Possum old pal, I'm just going to the bathroom." Somehow the touch of the cat, even the sound of her voice, comforted her.

She felt her way through the darkness to the door. Strange the way the reassurance she had felt from touching Poss vanished as soon as she stepped out into the black hallway. If she walked straight, she would come to the bathroom. She could switch on the light and this frightening night would disappear. The dark would be gone but she'd probably wake Grandma and then her chances of finding Jessie would be gone too.

The awful loneliness returned. She needed the doll. She couldn't explain it, had not recognized it at first, but there was an urgency that frightened her. She *had* to have it.

Meg did not go straight across to the bathroom. She turned right, towards the stairs. Grandma had taken Jessie downstairs.

It was even darker this way. She couldn't see the stairs at all. She might walk right off the top and go crashing down and break her neck—an arm or a leg anyway. Then she wouldn't be able to go back with Jessie. She could go, but she wouldn't be any use to Mother then. She might even slow them down so it took even longer to get to the homestead. Meg stood still. She should turn around, climb back into bed with Poss, and wait until daylight. Grandma would surely give Jessie back in the morning.

She hesitated, shivering a little in the unfriendly dark. But what if Lizzie woke up? Papa and the boys were busy with the wagon and Mother was moving the cattle up. Lizzie might find another badger or wander into the slough. The hummocky ground made it look safer than it was.

She moved cautiously forward, extending her foot an inch or two, pausing, feeling the way. She expected at any moment to feel the air—the emptiness at the top of the stairs.

Squeeeak! The sound filled the dark hall. It seemed to go right up Meg's leg, through her body, and echo from the top of her head. The squeaky board! How could she have forgotten it?

She waited, standing stone-still. Expecting Grandma's light to go on down the hall, Grandma's voice to call out.

Nothing. The darkness was quiet—still. Meg lifted her foot, half expecting the screech again.

Third board from the top, she remembered. Carefully she slid her foot forward until her toes found the edge. She lifted the other foot over the squeaky board. Holding the bannister she began to go down the stairs. Why had she never counted the steps? There was a coat rack at the bottom that wasn't any too steady—she mustn't bump into that.

At last, carefully, slowly, she reached the bottom. She stood for a moment holding the newel post. She couldn't see anything here, although a faint light showed through the kitchen door. That gave her some direction, but she knew there was a wobbly little table alongside the staircase just between it and the kitchen. The table was bad enough if you bumped it, but it held a small top-heavy lamp and two or three of Grandma's African violet plants.

Meg shuddered at the thought of bumping the table and knocking any or all of these things to the floor. It would be a disaster.

She moved a few steps away from the foot of the stairs, turned to face the dim doorway, and walked stealthily down the hall. She arrived breathless. Not from moving quickly, she realized, but just because she'd been holding her breath so long. Standing there, her hand clutching the doorframe, Meg wondered if it would be safe to turn on a light. Better to risk that than to knock something over, and besides, how could she possibly look for the doll when she couldn't see?

She closed the door behind her, holding the knob so that there was hardly any sound as it clicked shut. She flicked the switch and light flooded the room. Meg stood blinking like an owl at sunrise.

Now where would Grandma put Jessie? She glanced quickly around the room. The kitchen table told her that Grandma had sat for a while with a pot of tea. There was her gardening magazine lying open beside the empty cup. No clues from that. If the doll was damp Grandma might have tried to dry her out. The oven? Meg opened the door but it was empty. Grandma would hardly put a fragile doll in the clothes dryer. Where else could she air something?

Then she spotted the towel lying on the hot air vent behind the table. Of course! Grandma always used to dry Meg's boots upside down there so the hot air would go inside them. Mind you, that was long ago when Meg used to get them full of snow playing outside, but maybe . . . It seemed like a good idea, but when she checked inside the towel all that was there was the tattered dress.

She searched the cupboards too, every one, but the doll was not there. Meg felt like crying but she didn't dare make that much noise. She was feeling cold and shaky now. Hopeless.

Quietly she switched off the light and opened the door. She wasn't sure how she got back across the hall and found the foot of the stairs but she did it. She felt so tired. Tired and discouraged. She would wait until it started to get light. Besides, she needed to warm up now, she was so very cold.

Somehow she managed to get back across the squeaky board and felt along the hall for her bedroom door. At last, the bed. Grateful to be able to crawl between the covers, she pushed Poss over and lay on his warm spot. I hope Lizzie's okay, she thought, lying very still. I'll just shut my eyes for a little while.

Meg slept fitfully, tossing and turning so much that every now and then Poss would reach out a paw and give her a swat in disgust. Sometimes in her dreams she and Lizzie were being swallowed down a badger hole, sometimes they were in the slough and Meg was trying to haul Lizzie over the hummocky ground. Once, she moaned in her sleep and woke herself up.

At last, by the dawn half-light she sat up. She could see fairly well now and she had to find Jessie. She knew Grandma got up early too so there wasn't much time. Not enough time to search the whole house the way she'd searched the kitchen.

If only there was some kind of doll-detector, like a metal-detector, Meg thought. Or a bloodhound that tracked dolls.

Old Possum stretched himself and rubbed against her and Meg reached out to pat him. It was nice to have him sleeping with her again.

She looked at him and began to smile. What about a tracking cat?

She picked the heavy cat up and started out of the bedroom. Even carrying him she managed to avoid the squeaky board and soon she was downstairs. She'd do the living room first, she decided.

Holding Poss out in front of her she moved around the room. It wasn't easy. The cat hated being carried and especially thrust out like that, shoved towards cushions and under chairs. Every now and then she had to sit and pet him to calm him down.

She finished the living room and the dining room. She was about to go back upstairs and risk doing the upstairs rooms, but Possum was so heavy she sat for a minute on the cedar chest in the hall before beginning the climb.

The big cat stiffened in her arms. The chest! Of course! Grandma had probably put Jessie back in the chest for the night, thinking the odour would be lost that way.

Meg held Possum's nose against the narrow slit along

the top of the chest. Instantly he hissed and was gone, leaving three bloody claw tracks on her arm.

Meg opened the chest to meet Jessie's gaze. The eyes didn't look the slightest bit grateful. Rather there was a 'What took you so long?' expression that Meg found rather hard to take as she licked her sore arm, picked the doll up, and hurried towards the stairs.

She was so anxious to get to bed that she almost stepped right on the squeaky board. Avoiding it at the last minute made her stumble and bump into the wall. She stood very still, not breathing. Had Grandma heard the noise? Meg was close enough to her own door to slip in and be in bed before she was found out anyway.

She pulled the covers over them both, closed her eyes, and waited.

She was aware of voices whirling around her. Concerned voices. She recognized Papa's low rumble, ". . . too much for the poor lass," and Archy's: "Is she going to be all right?" Then Geordie's voice—soft, frightened: "She's so still . . ."

She could feel Mother's hand, gentle on her forehead. She opened her eyes.

They were all bending over her.

"Mooog!" Lizzie howled, trying to wriggle out of Archy's grasp to get to her.

"No Lizzie, you can't hug her, it might hurt her." There was concern in Archy's eyes. "I remember how it pained you so . . . to move or be touched when the fever first hit you back on the trail."

Meg sat up and held out her arms. "Not any more. That was just when I was really sick." So it was the same, she thought. The fever Mother talked about was rheumatic fever. Lizzie gave her a small hesitant hug that soon forgot itself and would have done a grizzly bear proud.

Meg looked around. She was in the wagon—they had lifted her in, quilts and all.

"Is the pain back, Morag, lass? We'll not travel more today if it is. Tomorrow's Sabbath so you'll have lots of rest."

Meg was shocked. "Oh no! The pain's gone . . . moving won't hurt me . . . really." It upset her terribly to think of them delaying because of her.

She had to convince them. "I'm fine, truly . . . I'll go herd the cows with Geordie. I should check on Buttercup . . ." She started to get up. "And he probably can't handle Evangeline by himself!"

Geordie was right on cue: "I can handle them fine without your help, and Buttercup's moving so fast now a midget couldn't keep up anyway!"

It worked. She could tell by the relief on their faces.

"Midget!" She tried hard to glare at Geordie with her usual enthusiasm. He was having trouble too, she noticed. As he turned to stomp away, she caught sight of a big grin.

Meg lay back on the quilts as the wagon bounced along. She wondered if it might not be less bumpy if she climbed up and sat on the seat with Mother and Lizzie.

"Morag! Lizzie's coming back with you for a wee while. We're going to keep moving 'til near dark. And," Mother's face twinkled a smile, " 'tis our last stop before we cross the river at Gabriel's Crossing."

Lizzie tumbled across the quilts to sit beside Meg. "You can hold Jessie Doll for a while," said Meg. I'm not going to, she thought.

Lizzie rocked the doll. "Story! Lizzie and rabbit hole," she commanded. Meg laughed and began, a mixed-up story that was part *Alice in Wonderland* and part Lizzie in the badger hole. I'll bet I could tell my own Rosie O'Malley stories at this rate, she thought. She felt good.

9

Meg was sitting on a log making butter. At least she'd been plunging the dasher of the wooden churn up and down, up and down into some thick cream. Her shoulders were beginning to ache when Geordie came along.

"I'll take a turn at that if you'll come and help me unload the chicken crates. It's a two-man job but Archy's busy so I guess one man and one midget can do it!"

That did it! Meg walked deliberately and quietly around Geordie—like a mongoose circling a snake. Geordie kept turning to face her, obviously baffled. When she had him where she wanted him, she stopped.

"Listen you!" She would have liked to grab him by the shirt and give him a good shaking, but since he was a foot taller than she was she decided against it. "I've just about had it with this midget stuff! I'm just the right size, so back off!"

To her surprise he actually did take a step backwards. There was a puzzled look on his face. Evidently poor sick Morag didn't talk like this. She'd show him.

She had him standing right where she'd planned, the log directly behind him. One good shove and he was over. Flat on his back in the rosebushes. Meg knew she'd better get ready to run but the expression on his face was too good to miss. Absolute astonishment! She couldn't help it. She laughed. Hard.

She knew she was probably going to be torn limb from limb but she couldn't stop. And Geordie was taking his time about moving. Just lying there, the strangest expression on his face. It seemed to be flashing from surprise to annoyance to something else she couldn't quite figure out. It only made her laugh harder. Running was out of the question now. She was doomed.

Except—except that now Geordie was laughing too. Rolling over out of the rosebush, getting up and— laughing. He looked delighted.

"You're better! You really *are!* Better than ever! Ever since you got sick you've been so meek and mild, it didn't even seem like you." He gave her an impish grin. "Now you're just like the old you—and then some!" The grinning face was close to hers now.

"But you're still a midget!" and he yanked her braid and raced away.

When Meg curled up with Lizzie in the quilts that night she was tired, really tired. There had been more than the usual unloading they did each evening because tomorrow was Sunday. They were going to have a day of rest, Mother said.

It was a good thing, Meg realized, not just for the people but for the animals too. Buck and Bright would be able to pasture. Unlike the cows they didn't get a chance to grab mouthfuls of grass as they went along. Even if they had the chance, the trail was worn from all the wagons and carts that had come this way. As far as Meg was concerned she was glad mostly for Buttercup's sake. When she'd visited the calf after supper, the poor little thing was sleeping, hardly raising its head for her to pet, and ignored the handful of nice green grass she'd found for it.

Meg realized that her hands smelled of calf. Oh well, it was a nice comfortable smell. Not at all like barns, or manure.

She wiggled away from Lizzie's elbow that was poking her in the ribs and fell asleep.

Later that night she felt the covers being tucked around her, and something in her arms, but she only snuggled into the warmth of the quilt and slept again.

Grace Cameron was in the kitchen, polishing the toaster absentmindedly. She was staring at the telephone on the wall, trying to make up her mind whether she should call her daughter at work. Twice she set down her cloth and started for the phone, then turned back. Once she even picked up the receiver and raised her finger to dial but changed her mind and returned to her already gleaming 'oaster. She was still polishing when the phone rang.

"Hello, Mother! How are things?"

"Janet, I'm so glad you called. I'm worried about Meg. I don't want to upset you, and of course it could be nothing . . . but she does seem to be sleeping a lot."

Her daughter's voice was puzzled. "But surely that's what we want? She needs lots of rest."

"Yes, I know . . . It's just that she . . . it's such a strange sleep. She seems to be stiff . . . she obviously *is* stiff. She doesn't complain about it but . . . she *is* walking very slowly. I was going to tell Mark about it last night when he was here but I didn't want to bother him."

"Why not? He's got to accept some responsibility!"

"I'm not sure it's a bad sign. It's probably just part of the recuperation. Still . . ."

"We can ask the doctor tomorrow. That's why I'm phoning. She has an appointment Wednesday at two o'clock. I'm going to take the day off and drive out in the morning." Janet Thompson paused. "If you like I can come straight out from work tonight and stay over, just to see how things are."

"That would be nice, dear." She took a deep breath. "And Janet . . . I think you should tell her . . . about you and Mark . . . She seems to be worrying about something. Maybe it would be better if you talked to her."

There was a sigh. "I suppose we've got to tell her, but I want both of us to do it. Together." Grace Cameron could hear her daughter's voice harden. "Mark thought we should wait until she was stronger. Really, Mother, as long as she's staying with you it doesn't make any difference whether Mark and I are together or not."

"I suppose not, except that . . . well, she seems so preoccupied. As if she's worried about something. I'm sure she senses there's a problem . . . and . . . sometimes it's easier to know where you stand." I've probably said too much, she thought. "We can talk about it when you come out anyway."

She hung up, glancing at the kitchen clock above the sink. Nearly noon. And Meg still sound asleep. This is the latest she's slept since she arrived. Of course, Janet is right—the whole point of her being here is to get lots of rest. But it wasn't the amount of sleep really, it was the *way* Meg slept that bothered her. She'd noticed it several times now.

This morning when she called and there was no response she decided to let Meg sleep. Even when she'd gone in to check from time to time she'd resisted the temptation to shake her granddaughter, wake her from the strange coma-like sleep. That was it. That was what was frightening her. It was like a coma. As if Meg wasn't there anymore.

Morbid thoughts—I mustn't even think such nonsense. She rinsed her teacup in the sink and turned purposefully. I'll just check on her again. I could use the excuse of taking Jessie back to her.

But when she opened the old cedar chest she found to her amazement that the doll was gone.

Meg was surprised to wake up in the soft bed. She had deliberately left Jessie where Lizzie had been playing, but there was the doll and there was Grandma standing over her, looking worried.

"You've missed breakfast, Meg love. It's almost lunchtime." She pulled back the covers. "Are you all right?"

Meg pushed the doll over against the wall. She sat up and started to climb out of bed. She did it smoothly; she wasn't as stiff today. "I'm fine, Grandma."

I'd better get to the bathroom and wash before Grandma smells Buttercup, she thought. She's got a nose like a bloodhound.

But Grandma Grace had other things on her mind. "Meg? How did you end up with Jessie?"

Meg had been wondering the same thing. She was sure that the doll was not in the pile of quilts when she and Lizzie went to sleep.

"I don't know, Grandma," she said, puzzled. Too late, Meg realized what Grandma meant: How did Jessie get out of the cedar chest and into your bed? "I . . ." Now how am I going to explain how I found the doll and why I wanted to? Meg wondered. "I . . ." Her voice trailed off. "I have to go to the bathroom!" She hurried across the hall.

"Never mind, Meg, don't worry about it," said Grandma, following her. "Come along downstairs as soon as you can." And she left Meg and turned to go down the stairs.

"Now the child's walking in her sleep!" she mumbled.

I guess there's no harm in Grandma thinking I'm sleepwalking, thought Meg, using lots of soap on her hands. Especially if it means I don't have to think up an excuse about Jessie. She smiled—at least Poss isn't going to tattle on me!

"Are you, Possum?" She bent to pet him before she started down the stairs. "Am I forgiven for last night?"

The old cat thumped down the stairs behind her.

The kitchen seemed cheerful in spite of the grey, threatening skies outside. Meg curled up on the window seat with Poss after she'd eaten. She was trying to see if there was enough blue in the sky to make a pair of Dutchman's breeches, but so far she'd only seen two very small patches. Meg decided that unless he was a very short skinny fellow, who wore his pants awfully tight, there was no possibility of it clearing up today.

Grandma didn't seem to be bothered by the gloomy day. "It's so nice to have you downstairs for a change, Meg. I have an idea! Why don't you get dressed and drive over to the store with me? It won't be too tiring and it would do you good to get some fresh air."

Meg hated to move. It was the kind of day she preferred to spend curled up indoors.

"Of course," Grandma said, looking pleased, "it's really because I want to show off my favourite granddaughter!"

Meg laughed. "I'm your *only* granddaughter!" She gave Grandma a hug as she went to get dressed.

10

Grandma made chicken for supper. Meg decided that it was coarser and less juicy than prairie chicken.

"You're not eating very much, Meg." Janet Thompson was trying not to pay too much attention to the way her daughter was delicately moving the cut-up pieces of chicken from one side of her plate to the other. So far, five pieces had been casually poked under the mashed potatoes and gravy, three under the creamed corn, and only two had actually found their way into Meg's mouth. The salad had been given a few listless stabs and spread around a little but none had been eaten. "Aren't you hungry at all?"

Meg put her fork carefully down on her plate. With any luck Grandma would take it away before it was examined too carefully.

"Not really," she said. She wished supper would be over. If her mother hadn't been coming tonight she would have been in bed by now. In bed with Jessie and back with her other family. Mother had said that they were going berry picking. She didn't want to miss that. No travelling for a change. She was probably missing out on the berry picking right now.

"I suppose you're not likely to work up much of an appetite when you're not doing anything." Her mother sounded doubtful. "Still, I worry about you losing weight if you don't eat enough."

"I've got an idea. Why don't we weigh Meg every day just to make sure she's holding her own?"

Meg gave Grandma a smile of relief. "Good idea!" The smile faded. What if she turned out to be *gaining* weight instead!

Grandma was clearing the dishes away. "What about a wee little piece of pumpkin pie, Meg? Would you have room for that? I know it's your favourite."

It was. And she knew her mother would never believe it if she turned that down. "Mmmm, yes please!"

She managed the first two bites with enough enthusiasm to see the worried look leave her mother's face. Good. Meg relaxed. She might even get another bite down if she took her time.

"Oh Meg . . . tomorrow, after the doctor's office . . . Guess what? We'll be going out for lunch with your dad . . . Have a nice talk." Janet Thompson's voice trailed off.

The piece of pie in Meg's mouth seemed to expand as she chewed it. She couldn't possibly swallow—it was stuck there.

So this was it. A nice talk. It was going to happen. She dropped her serviette and while retrieving it managed to spit out the pie that was choking her.

"That's nice," she said, trying to keep the 'nice' from sounding fierce.

She sat for a minute longer, then picked up her plate and stood up. "Is it all right if I take my pie up to bed with me? Finish it off while I'm reading, I mean?"

Her mother and grandmother were already clearing the table, stacking the dishes at the old-fashioned sink.

"Of course you can. I'll get your plate later," said Grandma.

"I suppose so, Meg, just don't get crumbs in bed," said her mother. They spoke together and then burst out laughing.

Meg left eagerly. Their talk followed her up the stairs.

"Wonderful how much that child reads! It'll be a shame when your TV set is fixed."

"It is nice to be able to enjoy reading so much." Grandma's voice was thoughtful. "I remember when I was a child my parents were always saying: 'Get your nose out of that book.'"

". . . and go outside and get some 'roses in your cheeks!'"

They were both laughing as Meg climbed the stairs. Meg smiled too. Roses in your cheeks was another of the family sayings—one of the stories Grandma often told.

Meg went straight to the bathroom. She had to get rid of the pie and she knew she couldn't hold another mouthful. It *was* a shame to waste it. Too bad she couldn't take it back for Geordie. She could just see his face if she could. He'd be so pleased!

She carefully cut the pie in mouth-sized pieces, flushing the toilet as she dropped them in one by one. That way the plate would look natural, not clean as if it had been scraped. She saved a bit of the crust and mashed it around with her fork.

'I've become a very sneaky person,' she thought. It wasn't a nice feeling. 'And a pretty good actress.' She remembered her convincing enthusiasm for the pie minutes earlier. It cheered her up. She moved in an elegant, actress-like walk across the hall. 'Perhaps I'll be a star someday!' Just as she was about to bow grandly to future fans, she remembered. Tomorrow.

She set the plate carefully on the bedside table and climbed sadly into bed. It was no fun thinking about the future now.

She sat for a while staring into Jessie's eyes. They

weren't threatening today. Meg gazed back into them. And felt calm.

"And then again perhaps I'll just be a pioneer . . ." she said out loud and lay down beside the doll.

She picked up the book that she was pretending to read. *Midnight is a Place* was one of the favourites she had brought from home. She'd ready it many times and she'd be reading it for real now if she wasn't always in a hurry to go to sleep. Having a book open on the bedside table as if it was being read was one way to keep Grandma from noticing how much sleeping she was doing.

Meg moved ahead a few chapters and let the book fall, just as if she'd fallen asleep reading. She didn't bother to pull up the covers all the way and she left the light on. With any luck at all Grandma and Mum wouldn't look in for an hour or two and they would think she'd been reading all that time and had just fallen asleep. She held Jessie casually, wanting it to look as if her arm had fallen accidentally over the doll as she slept.

When she woke up she was on the quilts in the wagon. Judging by the light it was late afternoon.

She had obviously missed lunch and maybe the trip to pick berries that Mother had promised as an afternoon treat. She set Jessie carefully on a box so she wouldn't be bounced out when they moved the quilts for the night and crawled out of the wagon. The camp was deserted.

It always amazed her how quickly each new campsite felt like home. She realized now with some surprise that it was the people, not the place. Now, among all the familiar things in the empty camp, she felt very alone. Lonely.

"Morag?" A voice was calling her from over by a wagon on the other side of camp. She could see a lady bending over a basket and from the sound of it there was a baby inside. She went over.

"I told your Ma that I'd watch out for you. I'm Mrs. Graham. We're crossing tomorrow too."

Meg moved closer. She could see a dimpled baby waving and kicking in the basket.

"Your folks just left for berry picking." She pointed. "There . . . over yonder rise. They'll be on the riverbank below. If you go up I expect you'll see them."

Morag felt a swell of relief. "Thank you!" She turned and began to run up the slope, the dry prairie grass crunching under her feet.

"Come back if you don't see them. You can stay with me," the woman called.

Morag just waved in reply. It was good to run, the sun warm and friendly on her back. She topped the rise in no time.

For an instant the lonely feeling returned, but then she saw them. Scattered below her—her family. Mother and Lizzie were closest, picking at some scrubby bushes low enough that even Lizzie could reach the berries. Archy and Geordie, tin pails hanging from their belts, were further down the bank where the bushes were taller and more heavily laden.

And there below, the river. She knew that all they had to do after they crossed the river was to cross the Saskatchewan Valley between the two rivers. The two rivers were really the north and south branches of the Saskatchewan River, Meg knew. And then . . . then, Fort Carlton and the homestead. She could see Mother looking into the distance already and knew she was yearning to be settled at last. Meg started down the bank towards them.

Lizzie saw her first. "Moog! Moog coming!" The fat legs began to run. The berry-streaked smile made Meg laugh. It was good to be Morag again, she thought, as she ran towards Lizzie.

Picking berries with Lizzie was not the most efficient way to fill your pail, Meg decided a short while later. For every two berries she put in, the chubby hand seemed to take three out. Meg soon despaired of making much of a contribution to the large wooden bucket that held their combined pick. Mother, in spite of Lizzie's help, had managed to empty her pail into the bucket and Archy had come up twice with his pail brimming just since she'd arrived. Geordie seemed to be picking more slowly.

When he arrived at last to empty his pail Meg stuck out her tongue at him by way of greeting. He returned it automatically.

"Look Lizzie, Geordie's tongue is blue like yours!" She had tricked him. Lovely. Somehow he'd managed to pop the berries in and not get his lips blue, but trust Geordie not to be able to keep his mouth shut and give himself away!

Geordie's guilty tongue led to Archy demanding a tongue inspection to see who was the best berry picker.

"Mother!" they chorused in shocked tones when she opened her mouth and reluctantly stuck out her tongue. There were the tell-tale blue stains.

As far as Meg was concerned that meant Archy was the champion. Much as she loved saskatoons, she couldn't squeeze even one in, not while she still felt stuffed with pumpkin pie. Besides, he had contributed most to the now-filled bucket. But he claimed only a tie and held her hand up in a victor's stance.

"Three cheers for the winners!"

"Three cheers for the best berry eaters!" yelled Geordie, grabbing Lizzie and rolling around on the hillside until the screams of laughter drowned out the cheers.

They sat there afterwards enjoying the late afternoon sunshine. Although the sky was clear, there was a haze in the valley and it smelled faintly of smoke. To Meg that was just the way late summer ought to smell, even though the breeze blowing up from the valley was unusually warm, almost hot.

They were all strangely silent. Lizzie sprawled, at last,

with her head in Mother's lap. Geordie tickled an ant with a blade of grass as it tried to scramble over a clump of dirt.

"It's a fine, happy day, Mother."

"Aye, Archy. 'Tis the kind of day to hold in your memory to warm and cheer the days that will come along that are not so fine, nor so happy."

Meg caught the look of tenderness in Mother's eyes and had to look away. She was surprised at herself. She was getting the same bursting feeling in her chest from being happy, that she'd only had before when she'd been sad. She realized her eyes were filled with tears.

She was glad when she saw Papa and Mr. Graham coming up the hill from the crossing. Now the talk was all praise of berries and plans for getting across the river in the morning.

The cattle would swim across, with Archy riding Pye to guide them. The oxen, cart, and wagon would go on the ferry with the family. It would probably take all morning to get everything across, what with their things and the Grahams, Papa said.

"Let's hope that everything gets across safely," said Mr. Graham in his gloomy way.

"Sufficient unto the day is the evil thereof," said Papa. It made no sense to Meg and she must have looked puzzled, for Mother explained quietly as they walked along.

"It means, lass, that each day brings its own troubles and we do ourselves no good to be pining about yesterday nor fretting about what tomorrow will bring. Just try to do our best with each day."

Meg thought she understood. "You mean we don't treat the bad moments the way we do the good ones ... holding on to them ... the way you told us just now?"

Mother laughed. "You've a way of putting things together, Morag, that I wouldn't have thought of. But you're right, lass. I think that's just what it means."

By the time they returned with Papa carrying the sleeping Lizzie and Archy carrying the berries, it was time to

81

start making supper. Rabbit stew again, but there'd be saskatoons and thick cream courtesy of Evangeline. Meg thought she just might have an appetite by the time she got all the berries washed and the leaves picked out.

Mother gave Meg a little hug as she bent over the saskatoons. "In the morning I'll show you how to make scones and we can put some berries in them and surprise everyone." It was a good idea.

Meg wondered how she could slip a pebble or two in the one Geordie got. A *special* surprise.

They got together with the Grahams after supper for a sort of Sunday service. She was very sleepy and the men's voices droned on and on in Bible readings. Then each said a very long prayer. Meg noticed that Mr. Graham seemed to be asking God for quite a bit, while Papa's prayer was mostly thanks for blessings of all kinds. Everything from her own recovery (again) and their 'safe journey thus far' to the weather and the trail, the health of the animals, and the 'good land that awaited their labours.'

Jessie was lying on the quilts beside her when Mother tucked Lizzie in and Meg curled up beside them. She could not have stayed awake another minute.

11

It was very early when she woke up in her soft bed at Grandma's; six o'clock by the clock on the dresser. Meg was grateful. It would give her a chance to get some real sleep. She was getting very, very tired again. She sat Jessie up in the far corner of the bed, put a pillow in front of her so that she couldn't accidentally touch the doll as she slept, and went back to sleep.

Meg was aware of whispering voices, Grandma's and Mum's.

"She's sleeping naturally enough now, Janet, but I tell you . . ."

"She *looks* fine . . ." Her mother sounded doubtful.

She opened her eyes. "Good morning. Did I sleep in again? What time is it?"

"Only seven thirty but your appointment is for ten thirty and we've got to allow an hour to get to Saskatoon and half an hour to get to Dr. O'Reilly's office, so it's up, up and away, if you're going to have a bath and breakfast!"

"I'll fix it now." Grandma was already on her way out the door. "Do you want one poached egg on toast or two?"

Meg groaned inwardly remembering all the saskatoons and thick cream she'd eaten only a couple of hours ago.

"Just one ... Maybe I'll just have a boiled egg instead, please." That way, she thought, I can leave quite a bit on the shell and Grandma won't notice.

Meg crawled reluctantly out of bed and put on the clothes her mother had brought. She certainly could use another hour or two of sleep. Maybe she'd get some in the car.

The restaurant they went to was very posh. Meg had been there with her parents once or twice before for special occasions. It was all white linen and flower arrangements and the waiter shook out her napkin and put it on her lap as if she couldn't be trusted not to put it on her head or something. Meg wanted to laugh and be happy because being here before had been happy. But it was like sitting in a lovely place knowing that soon someone would drop a bomb on it and you'd just be left sitting among the pieces.

She could hardly stand it. Listening to her mother talk in that 'company' voice, telling her dad about the report from the doctor.

". . . And you know how Grandma Grace has been worrying over her precious girl not eating enough and sleeping too much? Well, Meg is doing fine, much improved since her last visit!"

"That's my girl!" Her father reached around and gave Meg a hug.

"Dr. O'Reilly says that if the test results are as good as the physical examination she can start back to school next month."

Meg couldn't bear to look at them. She was grateful the waiter brought the soup just then so she had something to focus on.

". . . So that's just ten days before she'll be able to move back home."

The word 'home' seemed to fall with a thud in the middle of the elegant table. Her mother's voice wavered. Her dad took another roll and began buttering it very carefully even though he already had one. Meg stirred her soup. It was all she could do. Not even soup could have got by the lump, the terrible, hurting lump in her throat. Here it was. Now.

They both began talking then.

"We've decided . . ." ". . . best for all of us . . ." ". . . still love you . . ."

Words piled up around Meg until she wanted to flail at them with her arms and drive them away. Somewhere. Anywhere.

"Your mother is going to keep the house . . ."

". . . every other weekend with your father."

". . . keep your room . . . won't have to change schools . . ."

". . . summer holidays with your father."

". . . every other Christmas with your mother."

She couldn't bear to look at them. So earnest. So . . . so . . . concerned. So final.

"Stop!" Meg hardly recognized her own voice. A moment ago she was sure she couldn't have spoken because of the lump, but now she was getting mad and the lump was gone.

They stopped talking. So did the people at the next table, but Meg didn't care.

"You make it sound so . . . so . . . easy! It's not. That's me you're talking about. You've got me scheduled. Here . . . there . . . back . . . forth." She was feeling calmer now. Trying not to notice the looks on their faces. Astonishment? Alarm? Confusion?

"You can't divide me up like the furniture—Mum gets the piano, Dad gets the stereo. Only one child? Just split her down the middle. I'll have the weekday part, you take what's left of her on weekends . . ."

She wished her parents didn't look so stricken but she couldn't stop yet, not until she'd finished, if only her anger lasted long enough. The way they were looking at her made her want to cry. And the lump was back.

"You can't split me up! I love you both . . . all the time . . . not one during the week and one on the weekend!" The lump was back. She felt as if she was choking. She couldn't finish, couldn't tell them what it would be like to be a ball going back and forth. Catch . . . she's on your side . . .

"I'm not a ball," she burst out, ". . . not furniture . . . I'm Mor . . . Meh . . ." She stopped. Who *was* she anyway? "I'm ME!" she finished. And then sat there wishing she could disappear.

Nobody said anything. The waiter brought the food. Meg welcomed the interruption. Her dad was pulling another bun apart and he still hadn't eaten the other two. Her mother stared at the fettucine with clam sauce as if it was an invasion from Mars.

The waiter left. Still nobody said anything, although her father cleared his throat once or twice. Meg noticed there were tears running down her mother's cheeks splashing into the fettucine.

"We didn't know any other way to tell you . . ."

"We thought it would be easier for you if everything was planned." Her dad seemed to be having a coughing spell.

They don't know what to do any more than I do, Meg thought, amazed. Maybe even less than I do. They had to make the decision; I just have to do the best I can, like with the cow, or the badger. She was surprised at how calm she felt.

"We should eat our lunch," she said, remembering the beans and bannock. "Not everyone is lucky enough to have a meal like this!"

Her parents looked perplexed, then laughed. But it was a nervous kind of laughing and an awkward lunch after all. Nobody had dessert.

Meg didn't get a chance to sleep in the car on the way

home. As soon as she said good-bye to her dad and went to climb in the back seat her mother made her move into the front of the car. "So we can talk," she said.

But she didn't, she just drove. And Meg sat there. Waiting.

It seemed to Janet Thompson that the silence in the car wasn't quiet at all, but loud and getting louder. She was frantically going over opening lines, and as fast rejecting them as being too glib, too authoritarian, too . . . contradictory. At work she knew exactly how to cope with the difficulties of administration. Ask her to organize a conference, a workshop, anything, and she would have lists made, lines of authority drawn up, jobs delegated. That was how she'd arranged things at home too. Everyone had a job to do and did it. Except somehow it had gone wrong. Somewhere along the way she hadn't noticed that she and Mark didn't want the same things and so her plans were useless. She sighed. It was easier at work. Goals were set, everybody agreed, and then worked for it. Meg was looking at her in a strange way. She moved over to the centre seat belt to give her mother a sort of hug but she didn't speak.

The trouble with being a planner, Janet thought, is that you forget other people need to have plans too.

"I'm sorry, Meg. Your father and I . . . we should have told you sooner." She put her arm around Meg for a moment, trying to keep her voice steady. "I should have talked to you. I just didn't know how."

They were almost out of the city now, past the airport and the motels, onto the highway to Grandma's.

"To tell the truth," she tried again, "I've been so busy worrying about legal things, and how I'm going to keep the house and pay the mortgage . . . and . . . well, all those things you have to face in a divorce, that I tried to put off what was hardest of all. Thinking about what it would do to your life."

They pulled into a service station for gas, and she blew

her nose before she continued. "It's like . . . it's as if your house burns down or something. You have to figure out where you'll sleep and what you'll wear and you get caught up in the little details so much that you forget that everything's changed and your days will never be quite the same again." She realized suddenly that not only was this true, but that she had welcomed this aspect of it. Had relished being able to organize those things. She could control the details, and being busy kept her from having to think about those things that were out of her control. The future that had altered so much from her careful plans.

Meg wished she could think of something to say. She wanted to say, 'It's okay Mum, I understand.' But she didn't and she couldn't.

She watched her mother walking over to pay for the gas, her yellow suit and flowered blouse bright in the dull afternoon. She remembered how when she was little she'd always thought her mother was perfect. Never a hair out of place, always wearing beautiful clothes and never, never losing her temper and yelling like other kids' mothers did. Like Mary Poppins—practically perfect in every way. It was strange to see her nervous and unsure of herself. Hesitant. Frightened, perhaps?

Meg thought of what she'd said about the house burning. She could picture that. Coming home from school and finding just a charred shell of a house, the way they showed fires on the news on television. Everything gone. No clothes, no bedroom, and never the same clothes or bedroom again. She was beginning to understand. But you could manage, Meg thought. Some people managed with just a few things they could carry in a wagon and a cart.

Her mother got back into the car and drove carefully back onto the highway. Meg could see she was swallowing again and her eyes were bright but there were no tears.

Meg remembered how angry she'd been in the

restaurant because it seemed as though everything was so easy for her parents. As if they just calmly planned everything and then handed it to her, all done. Finished. Now she realized it hadn't been like that at all for them, but it didn't make her feel much better. She felt very tired.

She wanted to blot it all out. Forget it. She closed her eyes. They were nearly at Grandma's and all Meg wanted to do was get Jessie and escape.

Grandma was standing in the doorway. She didn't say anything, just looked at Meg's teary eyes and gave her a long hug.

"I think I need some hot, nourishing broth, Grandma," was all she could whisper as she hurried for the stairs.

But when Grandma arrived with the cup, Meg was already holding the doll, sound asleep.

12

"Morag's made scones! We can use them for ammunition to keep the wolves away from camp!"

Meg smiled sweetly at Geordie as she held out the plate. She'd had a bit of trouble passing it around and keeping Geordie's special scone from being taken. Archy had almost taken it, but she'd turned the plate in time and he'd had another. Now it was Geordie's turn. She'd chosen the biggest for the Geordie special. Naturally, he'd pick the biggest. He did.

He bit into it. Meg edged back around the log and handed the plate to Mother. She'd given some thought to her escape route. If she ducked behind the wagon she could double back along the trail and into the bush where the cattle were and hide there.

Geordie was chewing contentedly. "Doesn't exactly melt in your mouth. What the . . . That's no berry!"

Meg left. She could hear his shout: "Rocks! Mother, she's put rocks in my scone!" and Archy's hoot of laughter, and then running feet. By then she was in among the cattle. She crouched down between Evangeline and the calf. The footsteps were coming closer but she didn't dare look. Then she didn't hear anything. He must have run on down the path. She waited a minute longer and peeked around Evangeline.

"Aha!" He was right there. Waiting. And she couldn't possibly outrun him now.

"The cat has finally got the mouse!" Geordie was enjoying himself as Meg backed slowly around the cow. Rubbing his hands together, laughing in his most evil manner.

Over his shoulder Meg could see Papa and Mr. Graham coming down the trail. Stall. She had to stall. Buttercup rubbed against her and she petted her and pushed the calf between them.

"Mercy! You wouldn't hurt an innocent calf!"

"No, but there'll be no saving a guilty cook!"

"Geordie! Come here, lad!" Papa's voice had never sounded so beautiful to Meg. She ducked under Evangeline's neck. A little distance wouldn't hurt. "We're going to start packing up now. Mr. Fisher can take our wagon on the ferry. Come along and help your mother, Morag lass."

Meg moved gratefully over to walk beside Papa, giving Geordie a big triumphant smile.

She'd only gone a few steps when she felt the first pebble hit her shoulder. Then another. That stung! She glared back at Geordie. He looked innocent and pretended to study the path. She turned and moved a few steps ahead of Papa. This time the pebble bounced off her back right in front of him.

"Geordie, are you throwing pebbles at your sister?"

"No sir," said Geordie innocently, "just berries."

They arrived at the camp to find Archy and Mother busy loading the wagon. Meg quickly went to help Mother who gave her the twinkly smile as they tied the boxes in place.

"Seems your scones made a big impression on everyone today!"

Before long they were ready to move. The air still had

that smoky early autumn smell but the day seemed to Meg to be even warmer than it had been yesterday. Maybe, she thought, that's a good sign. We'll have a late fall and good weather to build the house.

"Whoa!" The wagon stopped in a muddy, rutted approach to the river.

"Where's the ferry?" she asked Papa.

He looked at her, puzzled, and pointed straight ahead of them. Meg was shocked. She hadn't been expecting the Vancouver Island ferry, but she'd thought that those boards floating in front of them were some kind of makeshift approach, where the real ferry landed. This was just a raft and not a very big one at that! Surely they weren't going to . . .

They were. Archy was already driving the pony and cart onto it. The ferryman, Mr. Fisher, was putting blocks under the wheels as Archy unhitched Pye, led him back to land, and mounted.

She was watching the ferry sway as the Grahams' cart came on, wondering if the whole thing would sink, when she realized that the cattle were already in the river, fording it a bit downstream from them.

"Buttercup! Where's Buttercup?" The water was much too deep for her. Meg left the wagon and ran along the edge of the river. Then she recognized Evangeline already well out into the river. The lead cattle were swimming now, following a strange cow she supposed was one of the Grahams' herd. There was Archy, on Pye, guiding them. The pony was swimming too, his nose just above water, his tail streaming behind him in the muddy river.

"Archy!" She knew even as she called that it was useless. Then she saw the calf. At its mother's side pressed close by the current. Nose out like the others. It was swimming! Clever Buttercup! No lessons or anything. Meg was impressed.

There was another rider in the water now bringing up

the last of the string of animals. She didn't recognize the horse but there was no doubt about the rider. There'd be no putting up with him now. Even from here he was looking pleased with himself. He waved to her. Show off. She hoped the horse would dump him in the river and wipe that silly clown grin off his face.

It didn't. By the time the last animals were swimming, Archy had the first ones already heading up the trail to pasture and rest. And Buttercup was walking along at her mother's side. Looking cuter than ever after her bath.

By the time Meg came back from watching the cattle, the ferry had somehow crossed the river and was now unloading on the other side. Archy had returned from driving the cattle up the trail and was hitching Pye back onto the Red River cart. Mother and Lizzie were sitting in the sunshine on a large rock, watching.

"There you are, Morag lass. We'll sit here until the scow returns and the men get the oxen and wagon loaded."

"Did you see Buttercup swimming? Wasn't she great? I didn't know she could swim."

"It's wonderful, isn't it? The way the Lord gave the animals the sense to swim without having to learn the way people do."

Meg realized Mother was holding Jessie out to her. "Lizzie kidnapped your doll again. You'd better carry her, in case she falls from the wagon."

The men were using oars to bring the scow across the river. Scow was definitely a more appropriate name than ferry as far as Meg could see. Except for the row of boards on two sides it still looked more like a raft than anything else. It landed quite a way down-river from them and the men hauled it back up to where the oxen waited patiently chewing their cuds.

Now they were driving the team onto the scow. There was a fair bit of 'Geeing' and 'Hawing' and Papa had to use the whip to get Buck and Bright onto the shaking boards. Once on, Papa removed the big wooden yoke from their necks, brought them back into the centre, and tied them to the side of the wagon.

Mother, Lizzie, and Meg stepped on then. Mother and Lizzie climbed into the back of the wagon to sit, legs dangling over the edge, but Meg decided to stand, holding onto the rear wheel. She'd pulled a nice handful of grass for Buck and as she fed him, avoiding that long, rough tongue, she wondered that she'd ever been afraid of such a gentle giant.

The men pushed off from shore and Meg moved over to the other wheel, closer to the edge, so she could watch the river eddying beside the raft. Suddenly the current caught them and they were moving faster, swept out in midstream, turning . . . Meg felt dizzy. She grabbed for a tighter grip of the wheel and felt Jessie slip.

Her reaction was immediate. She didn't drop the doll but the cold fear that gripped her left her shaking and all thoughts of dizziness vanished.

She stared at the doll. The eyes mocked her. You need me, they seemed to say.

I don't, thought Meg. I can stay here and be a pioneer girl. I can't keep moving back and forth, being two people all my life!

She was glaring at the doll but the doll's calm face was stony and smug as ever.

Meg looked down at the murky water swirling around the side of the scow next to her feet. If she dropped the doll now . . . She could imagine the china face, blue eyes alarmed at last, floating briefly in the current, sinking slowly. Gone. She almost wished she could let go . . . but she couldn't. Not now. The doll seemed to taunt her—Morag or Meg, which will it be?

She heard Mother's voice then. Bringing her back. "Look at Geordie!"

The scow had turned. The rowing had pulled it, using the current, towards the shore just above the spot where the last of the cattle had come out of the river. There was

Geordie, his horse streaming water, coming triumphantly ashore. He was showing off again. Then the horse shook itself. Like a dog. Water flying everywhere and then . . . Geordie sitting in the mud. Looking more like a clown than ever! Meg could have cheered.

"He's not hurt, I hope." From Mother.

"Just his pride," said Papa, smiling broadly.

"How are the Mighty fallen . . ." quoted Mother.

"Ride 'em cowboy!" yelled Meg.

Geordie didn't look at them. He picked himself up and led the horse over to where Mr. Graham was waiting for it and followed the cows quickly up the trail.

Meg let Jessie drop onto the quilts in the wagon as they drove it up the bank and left the south branch behind.

It was still early. Mr. Graham came up in his doleful way to say good-bye before the Grahams turned north on the trail, heading for Prince Albert. Meg was not sorry to see them go.

"Are you sure you should be trying to reach Fort Carlton by nightfall? It'll be a long weary day, it's so warm and . . ."

Papa was impatient to be off. "Aye, we're eager to give it a try. The animals are rested and if we make it, it's our last day of travel. The boys are already well started with the cattle."

"God speed then." Mr. Graham finally turned to go. "Let us hope everyone on the trail has heeded the warning about camp fires . . ."

Meg didn't hear any more. She was running to catch up with Mother and Lizzie and the wagon.

13

The wind had been hot all day – drying the last traces
of green from the prairie grass, leaving it bleached and
flat. Meg thought the grass looked tired. As tired as she
was. She noticed it no longer sprang back to hide her foot-
prints or moved in its secret way with the wind, but lay
snug to the earth as if trying to hide from something.

She had not paid much attention to the hazy sky but
she sensed her parents' unease and noticed Archy's fre-
quent glances south in the direction they had come. At
first she'd thought it was just worry that they would not
reach the fort by nightfall, but now she wasn't sure. Archy
was driving the cart and Pye's white-rimmed eyes looked
even more frantic than usual. The cart's shrieks added
to the feeling. Tension. Something wrong.

Only Lizzie was behaving normally, wanting to get out
of the wagon and pick flowers. Meg could hear her howl
of protest when Mother insisted she stay where she was.

Meg ran breathlessly up and down her side of the herd
trying to keep them moving, and stay in line with
Geordie's side. Geordie was running back and forth hi-
yupping so that the cows were hard pressed to grab a bite
of grass as they moved along. Meg was glad that Buttercup and Evangeline were on her side. But when she

stopped and waited as the calf nursed, Geordie just kept his side moving, getting the herd strung out in a long line with Meg and Buttercup at the end, left behind in a little dip in the trail.

When the first white flakes began to fall Meg thought for a moment it was snow. Only for a moment, then she felt silly—of course it wasn't snow. She stared at some that landed on her hand. Warm. Ashes. Drifting down all around.

As Meg and the cow and calf came out of the gully to catch up with the others she saw the wagon and cart stopped ahead.

Archy and his parents stood in a cluster, then all moved at once. Archy helped Mother climb into the cart and handed her the reins. The piebald pony was restless but Mother held him in check, looking back towards Meg. She seemed to be arguing with Papa and Archy, shaking her head, waiting.

Then Papa was waving towards the herd, calling to Archy. And then she looked back. The way they had come. Behind her, on the horizon, the smoke was white and thick like clouds in the sky and lower down, where it was black, she could see patches of orange.

She turned. Archy was running towards her and Geordie. She began to run too.

She could hear Archy calling to Geordie, ". . . only a mile from the fort . . . Papa doesn't think we should try to make it with the cattle. They should be safe down there." He was pointing to a boggy area backed by a thick stand of willows just down the slope on Meg's left. She could see patches of water.

As he reached Meg he grabbed her in his arms and swung her ahead towards the wagon. "You and Lizzie are going to ride with Papa to the fort . . . run . . . hurry!"

"But you . . . the fire . . . Geordie, . . ." she panted.

He gave her a hug that turned into a shove. "We'll come after the fire passes . . . go, Morag . . . run!"

And she did.

When she was about halfway there, just when she was marvelling at how fast she was running, skimming the ground enough to make her believe the old saying about feet having wings, her chest began to burn, but she didn't slow down.

Only as Meg neared the wagon did Mother give in to Papa's urging. With one last anxious glance, she let the pony go. Tossing his head he set off, the screeching cart bumping along behind him.

Meg could see Lizzie, leaning out of the back of the wagon, waving. Her side was aching and she was holding it, but still running. Fast. Meg, who had never won a race in all her years of phys. ed., was sure she would have won this hundred-yard dash.

Now she was coming up to the back of the wagon, bent over, lungs aching, gasping for breath, and she felt Papa's arms swing her up into the back beside Lizzie. Felt the wagon start to move and heard the crack of the whip as Papa urged the oxen into a trot.

Meg lay there, coughing, panting, and waiting for the tightness in her side the loosen.

Lizzie patted her cheek. "Mooog, ride with Lizzie." Meg was grateful that the little girl resisted her usual urge for a bear hug. She was sure the weight of the two-year-old would have taken what little breath she had left. Lizzie was playing with something in the quilts as they bounced up the hill over the ruts.

Behind the wagon, Meg could see that the boys already had the herd down the hill and were circling round them trying to keep them in the wettest part of the bog. She could see more orange, see the shapes of the flames now as the wind swept the fire along.

Beside her Lizzie played, keeping slightly behind the crates piled along the sides of the wagon box. Meg caught a glimpse of Jessie and realized that Lizzie was trying to hide the fact that she was playing with the forbidden doll,

98

trying to sit her up on a ledge formed by the boxes. The wagon bounced and shuddered along, and Meg was grateful that Papa always insisted the boxes be tied down to the wagon's sides.

She sat up. They were on the flat crest of bank above a ravine and soon the trail would slant sharply down to the river flats below. Meg could see the logs of Fort Carlton and the strips of freshly ploughed ground that formed a firebreak around it. The pony and cart had already disappeared down the hill.

The wagon hit a rock and Meg landed with a teeth-jarring thud against one of the boxes. She turned to grab Lizzie before the child bounced out and as she did so she saw the doll topple off the box and fall into the dust of the trail.

"Lizzie! The doll!" Meg let go of the child, frozen in horror as she watched Jessie bounce, roll a few times, and come to rest inches from a large rock. Meg sat transfixed. The doll stared at her.

'You can't do anything,' it seemed to say. 'This is the end. Lose me and there is no more Meg!' Even lying there in the dust, being left behind, the doll's power was strong. A cold and helpless fear held Meg motionless. Staring.

Meg would never know whether Lizzie jumped or fell from the wagon. Whether the little girl lost her balance as she tried to hide from Morag's anger at the loss of her doll, or if another bump threw her out. Perhaps she went to retrieve the doll her sister cherished.

It happened so fast that it was only when she saw Lizzie sitting in the middle of the trail, face puckered ready to howl from the shock of the fall, that Meg even realized she was gone.

She didn't stop to think or speak. Suddenly the numbness left her and she was jumping, landing on her feet, almost falling, and then getting her stride as she ran back to Lizzie.

Whatever plans the child had for crying were cut short

when she saw her sister running towards her. She scrambled up and was off. Away. Back to the doll.

By the time Meg caught up with her and turned to run back to the wagon it was gone. Just disappearing over the edge of the bank, down the trail to the fort.

"Papa!" She started running awkwardly, holding child and doll. "Papa . . ." Her voice trailed off.

He didn't know they were gone. Had not seen them fall out. Might not even notice them gone until he arrived at the fort. The ashes were falling thicker now. She glanced behind her and saw the flames sweeping towards them.

Meg stood, holding Lizzie close. She knew they couldn't run the quarter of a mile down the hill fast enough to beat the fire to the fort on the flats. And it would be stupid to try to run back to where the boys were. The flames looked as though they were already past the place where the herd had gone down the bank.

There's only one chance, Meg thought.

"Hold my hand tight, Lizzie." She began to half drag, half carry the little girl down into the ravine. Straight down. Slipping down the steep bank, their dresses catching on the rosebushes.

Lizzie stumbled and fell, rolling on down the bank until she came to rest against a bush, still clutching the doll. Meg plunged after her, catching her up and rushing on, down to the bottom of the ravine.

She didn't dare look back up the bank. The smoke was much thicker and, now and then, along with the falling ash, bits of flaming grasses blew along in the wind and fell near them. Sometimes they went out, sometimes small fires would start where they landed. Meg didn't dare stop to try to stamp them out.

They were almost at the bottom. It looked marshy but she couldn't be sure if there was enough water. In the spring there would be a stream here, she thought, but now?

14

Meg's foot slithered on a root and a sharp pain shot up her leg. She was carrying Lizzie altogether now. She wasn't sure if the tears in her eyes were from the smoke or the pain in her ankle. Lizzie was crying. Not loud, just gasps, like hiccoughs, as if she couldn't get her breath well enough to really cry.

Then Meg's foot sank into the mud and she saw the small trickle of water. A creek, almost dried up after the long summer and dry weather, but some water.

Enough water for them to lie in. At least she hoped it was enough. She sat Lizzie down on the edge of a little pool and began tearing strips of cloth from her slip, glad that the old-fashioned petticoat was made of cotton and easy to tear. As she wet the cloth she realized that Lizzie was about to get her breath back enough to howl.

"Look Lizzie! Morag's going to wear a funny mask!" She placed the wet cloth over her mouth and nose. "Lizzie can too!" She kept talking, slowly, reassuringly. Lizzie eyed Meg doubtfully.

The clumps of burning grass that fell around them had ignited the grass on the other side of the ravine so that the fire crept along on both sides. Meg wet more petticoat and lay it on top of Lizzie's head to protect her hair from the falling grass.

"Let's play in the water, Lizzie!" Meg sat down in the middle of the little pool. It barely covered her lap. She began to splash water on herself, wetting her hair, her dress. Lizzie looked at her with horror. Taking a bath with your clothes on was something new.

"Lizzie too!" She threw herself into the water and came up sputtering. Meg play-wrestled with her, making sure her clothes and hair were wet, although the hot wind seemed to dry them both off so quickly they had to keep rolling in the water.

The fire was all around them now. The smoke thick above them. Meg was glad that the air along the bottom of the ravine was clear.

Lying there, looking up, it seemed to her that the whole world was on fire. There was no sky above, only smoke— heat pressing in on them, and the terrible roar of the fire. It was a noise unlike any Meg had ever heard. Loud, but not like jet engines. A deep sound, an animal sound. Like hundreds of lions all around them.

She wet the face masks again and they lay side by side on their backs, Lizzie's head on her shoulder, their heads in the water. She could feel the pull on her skin, the fierce heat drying the cloth over her face as the fire swept by.

And then it was gone. Moving down the sides of the ravine to the fort. In places on the bank, where the grass had started fires down below and then worked up the bank to the main one, the fire was burning against itself and making a sort of fireguard around them. On the ridge above Meg could see the fire still sweeping along the trail.

She sat there. Afraid to wonder how the boys had made out—had the bog been big enough to act as a fireguard and protect all the cows? She hoped Papa hadn't turned back and got caught by the fire.

She did not let herself wonder when, in the mad

scramble down the bank, Lizzie had dropped the doll. Meg didn't dare think where Jessie might be now.

Lizzie rolled about splashing happily in the mud beside her as Meg's eyes searched the blackened hillside for a patch of white—would it be white anymore?—a china face.

She wondered how long it would be before all the small fires were out and the ground cool enough for them to start for the fort, or for Papa to come looking for them.

And then it began to rain.

At first it was wonderful. Lovely cool drops on her parched face. She opened her mouth and let the rain cool her tongue, trying to gather enough to swallow.

The rain will put all the fires out, Meg thought. Then when it stops, I can haul Lizzie back up the bank and follow the ruts of the trail down to the fort.

But the rain only got heavier. The drops weren't refreshing anymore but hard and cold. They stung when they hit her face. She began to shiver.

Meg pulled Lizzie from the pool that was really just a mudpuddle now and looked around for some shelter. It was hard to see in the pelting rain and besides, she knew that any bushes that had survived the fire, if not smoldering, were not big enough to provide any protection. There was a large rock, a boulder near where she had turned her ankle. Perhaps that . . .

She'd forgotten her ankle but when she started up the bank, a stab of pain reminded her quickly enough. The boots she hated so much squished with water when she walked but they supported her ankle and she managed to get herself and Lizzie up to the rock. By then both of them were shivering.

The boulder was almost useless as far as shelter was concerned. It was half buried in the hillside and there was no overhang. Still, there seemed to be a dry spot on the leeside of it where they could sit. Meg felt carefully around for any still-smoldering spots on the blackened earth before she sat down with Lizzie. Her teeth were chattering uncontrollably now and the raindrops still beat at her face. Harder than before.

Cradling the little girl in her lap, her back against the rock, Meg noticed that the rock was warm. She was grateful for that, although she knew that the heat it held from the fire would not last long. Perhaps it would last long enough to keep them warm until the rain ceased.

Fear circled in the back of her mind. In late summer a cold rain could turn to sleet. It seemed to be getting darker too. Could she find the trail and follow it in the dark?

They huddled together against the rock. Lizzie was exhausted, mud-streaked and cold, but she didn't seem to be shivering as much as Meg was. It was that bone-cold feeling again. It seemed to take over so that the worries about rain, night, and being lost were floating off somewhere outside and all that Meg was aware of was the cold. The cold filled her. And it was growing darker.

She thought she must be dreaming now. She wasn't cold anymore. In fact she was warm, a little too warm. Lizzie nestled close to her, asleep. In her half-sleep Meg rubbed her hot cheek against the little girl's cool forehead. She was so hot. Sometimes she dozed and dreamt she was in the fire, she was so hot. And then she was no longer aware that the rain had stopped as she lay in the cold darkness. Nor of the little sister she was warming with her fevered body.

Nearby, on the other side of the big rock, in a place the fire had missed, lay the doll.

Jessie lay on her back, her china face white in the gathering darkness, her eyes still staring. Staring.

Pools of rainwater blurred the blue eyes and now and then a drop spilled down the doll's cheek.

15

It was not until the first light of dawn that the boys, bringing the herd along the trail to the fort, met the search party.

The muddy dresses blended against the black rain-washed bank, and the big rock, partly hid the girls so that the searchers did not see them at first. Not until they heard Lizzie's wailing.

"Mooog! Mooog! Wake up!" She howled as she poked her sister.

But Morag did not wake up, even as they carried the girls back to the fort. She only tossed and moaned and called for Jessie.

It was Geordie, left behind to drive the cattle, scrambling back down into the ravine to bring up the reluctant Evangeline and her calf, who noticed Buttercup sniffing at something behind the rock—something white.

He carried Jessie back to the fort and took her to his sister.

Morag was lying in one of the cots, turning and moaning while Mother bathed her face with cool water.

He watched for a few minutes. What was she saying? He could catch the odd word. "Home" and what sounded like "Mum ... Dad ... " and then, when she didn't respond when he said her name except to thrash about more wildly and call for Jessie, he put the doll in her arms.

She opened her eyes then and smiled at him. He smiled back. His face was smoke-blackened and his eyebrows were almost singed away, but he gave her his best grin.

"Here's your doll, Midget."

She almost managed a laugh looking at him. "Thanks, Clown," she murmured.

Morag closed her eyes and was still.

16

"Maybe you're right . . . we should just pack her into the car and take her to emergency."

Grace Cameron was pacing back and forth beside the bed, pausing every few minutes to feel the forehead of the motionless girl on the bed.

Her daughter out-paced her. Back and forth between the bed and the window.

"Mark should be here soon, it's been nearly an hour." She glanced from her watch to the clock on the dresser as if hoping that one of them would be lying and Meg had not really been stretched out beneath the covers so pale and still for such a long time.

"When did you first notice her this morning? . . . that she didn't respond?" It was a question Janet had asked every few minutes since she arrived.

"I looked in on her when I first got up . . . about seven, but I didn't call her or anything . . . just let her sleep. I called her later on . . . about nine thirty. I thought she should have breakfast. She didn't answer so I came and shook her a little. But she just wouldn't wake up. She often slept like that, not moving at all. I told you about it . . ."

Janet Thompson sighed. "I know, I know . . . I just didn't realize . . ." She started for the door, paused halfway and came back. "Mark will be here. He's always punctual. I used to think he was too damn punctual, but he'll be here and then we'll take her in . . . You're right, we'll have to take her to emergency so Dr. O'Reilly can see her."

She stopped pacing and stared at her daughter's face. Pale and still. Why didn't she move or moan or something? Her face was so white. Janet's gaze travelled to the doll Meg clung to. She remembered holding the doll when she'd been sick. Remembered drifting in and out of sleep, aware of the doll. In those days the doll's eyes had seemed to be always staring. Uneasy. As if searching for something. What? She stared at the doll. Strange that she'd thought it was a searching look in the doll's eyes. It wasn't at all. The eyes looked content now. Almost as if Jessie had found what she'd been looking for.

Grandma Grace sat on the edge of the bed holding Meg's hand. She smoothed Meg's hair away from her forehead, touching it gently, checking for a fever, shaking her head. Puzzled.

They both heard the car almost before it pulled up in front of the house.

Mark Thompson carried his daughter out to the car, wrapped in the blanket from the bed, still holding the doll, not moving. Meg lay in the back seat, her head on her mother's lap. Grandma Grace sat in front, turning every few minutes to look at her granddaughter. Nobody spoke until they were in the city, driving past the airport, and Janet Thompson's voice startled them.

"She's moving!"

Meg had turned, tried to stretch out, pushing violently against the blankets, the confines of the car seat. "Mum . . . Dad . . . Jessie . . . oh no!" She kicked out frantically.

"We're here, Meg! It's all right . . . we're here and you've got the doll, you've got Jessie. You're going to be all right."

Meg felt the doll in her arms, then heard the voices, the sound of the car, and opened her eyes. She was back . . . safe . . . home. "I was so cold . . . and then so hot . . ."

No, that was Morag. She closed her eyes again quickly because there were going to be tears. Lots of tears.

She felt her mother's hand on her forehead. "You're not hot now. But you frightened us. You were lying so still ... sleeping so long."

Meg nodded. She was remembering. Losing the doll, the fire, the rain ... "Lizzie," she murmured, struggling to sit up.

Grandma's voice. "Jessie? Do you mean the doll? She's right there."

Meg felt the doll pressed against her side. She couldn't quite sort things out. Was Lizzie all right? It had been so cold in the rain. She'd tried to keep the little girl warm ... she'd been so hot herself ... she couldn't remember. Then, feeling the doll in her arms, she remembered. A clown face, streaked and black—Geordie had found the doll and brought it to her.

The tears really were streaming down her cheeks now.

Then the car was stopped at emergency, her dad was bending over, gathering her up, carrying her. Somehow Jessie fell onto the pavement, was picked up, and carried in by Grandma.

The person most confused by the medical examination was Meg. She could understand why Dr. O'Reilly thought she was tired. She was. She felt like a worn-out shoe. Although Grandma's reaction when she heard the doctor's comment was indignant.

"How could the child be tired? She's been spending most of her time in bed, for heaven's sake!"

Meg caught a glimpse of her ankle, the one she'd twisted rushing down the bank, swollen and sore now. Her mother was already asking Dr. O'Reilly about it, pointing it out. Meg had an excuse ready—she'd banged it on the foot of the bed getting up to go to the bathroom in the night. But it wasn't needed. The doctor explained that swollen joints were a common aftermath of rheumatic fever.

Meg had been really worried about her hands. There were red blotches on them from the heat of the fire. But he explained that away as well. "We often see skin rashes afterwards too," he said.

There was a different kind of silence in the car on the drive back to Grandma's. Not exactly comfortable, although the tension and worry was gone.

Grandma was different. She sat very straight in the front seat, still holding Jessie, every so often straightening her shoulders as if she had been freshly insulted and exclaiming, "Tired indeed" or "Not enough rest? Ridiculous!"

Meg realized that she was going to have to be a super patient and face a veritable Niagara Falls of hot nourishing broth before Grandma would forgive the slur on her nursing care.

Meg was just dozing off, lulled by the hum of the motor and the warmth of the blankets and her mother's arm around her, when Grandma's puzzled voice brought her back.

"This doll's broken! There's a piece chipped off her foot . . . just the toe . . . but I'm sure it wasn't broken before. I wonder when that happened?"

Meg sat up. Grandma was right. The doll had had two whole feet the last time she examined it. It must have happened when Lizzie dropped Jessie out of the wagon. It could have struck a rock as it fell. Maybe it happened in the mad scramble down the hill—she'd dropped the doll then. Meg had a sinking feeling. Here was something she couldn't explain. She was frantically trying to make up something when her mother spoke.

"Didn't the doll fall out of the blanket when you lifted Meg out of the car, Mark?"

Grandma's voice was relieved. "Of course, I picked the blessed thing up myself. Too bad I didn't notice it at the time. I might have been able to glue the missing bit back on."

Meg settled back. Grandma was still holding Jessie. Now she could have a real nap. Dr. O'Reilly had been right about one thing—she *was* tired. Exhausted. She closed her eyes.

She woke up when her dad lifted her out of the car, but she just put her head on his shoulder and let him carry her up to bed. It was lovely to be back in the soft, comfortable bed. Grandma had a hot water bottle at her feet and some soup and toast on a tray almost before Meg had a chance to settle in. Her parents were sitting in the straight-backed chairs by the bed as Grandma fussed around.

"Now if that doctor had said Meg was suffering from malnutrition, I'd have been inclined to believe him. She hasn't been eating enough to keep a sparrow alive!"

"His eye is on the sparrow," Meg murmured, remembering one of Mother's quotations. She caught herself quickly when she noticed the astonished looks on their faces. "I read that somewhere ... I think ..." she finished awkwardly.

Grandma laughed. "You know, just for a moment you reminded me of my granny ... your great-great-grandmother. She was always a great one for quoting from the Bible."

"Maybe you've absorbed something from her doll, Meg," her father teased. "Grandma says you can't bear to be separated from it."

"Where is Jessie? Still downstairs?" Her mother got up. "I'll get her if you like."

Meg shook her head. "Not right now. Here comes Poss. I'll just cuddle him instead." The old cat leapt awkwardly onto the bed and purred up beside Meg.

"The tea'll be ready, if you two want some."

They got up to follow Grandma.

"Come back before you leave ... Mum ... Dad ... I want to talk to you. Poss! Lie down, you'll spill my soup!"

17

Meg woke up feeling cramped. For some reason she couldn't move her legs. Poss! That cat really was a bed hog. It was dark in the house although she could see faintly in the hall.

Meg pushed Poss over and stretched. She felt much better. Inside and outside. The talk with her parents had helped. Not that it had worked out the way she had intended.

She remembered them coming in together and sitting down. Looking rather nervous. And she'd started out the way she'd planned.

"I've been thinking, and there are some things I want to tell you both." She stopped then. They were sitting there, straight and still, looking for all the world like two kids in the principal's office and it threw her.

"It doesn't matter if your house burns down. I mean . . ." Her father had looked completely confused, her mother only a little less. "I mean . . . home is where the people you love are," she began again. They still looked puzzled. How could she explain the way each campsite on the trail had been transformed? Had become warm and cosy as a hug.

She tried again. "I can handle having you apart, as long

as you don't make me feel I'm supposed to be on one side or the other." They waited patiently as Meg tried to think of a way to explain that she didn't want to have to pretend she didn't love both of them just as much, even if they didn't love each other any more.

"I mean . . ." she hesitated. They were still—sitting, waiting. It just wasn't like them. Meg felt confused. "I mean, I can handle it," she finished lamely. It wasn't what she'd meant to say but she knew as she said it that it was true. Badgers, cows, and prairie fires were not things she'd had to face and yet when the time came, she'd managed, hadn't she?

There were lots of other things she'd wanted to say, not scream the way she had in the restaurant, but she didn't get a chance because both of them had started to speak at once.

"I don't think we realized . . . really thought about it from your point of view . . ." her father began.

"We didn't recognize you'd have to figure things out for yourself . . . or even that you could do it," added her mother.

"You're really quite a girl, Meg baby. Should have given you more credit!"

Maybe the talk hadn't really solved anything. She had the feeling her parents were still worrying about her being sick and didn't want her thinking about anything else. She got out of bed.

She knew there'd be some tough times ahead. So why did she feel so much better? Why wasn't she as worried as she had been?

"Sufficient unto the day," she said with a smile. Remembering.

She crossed to the dresser where Jessie sat. Last night when Grandma brought the doll upstairs Meg hadn't wanted to sleep with it. She knew now she couldn't flip-flop back and forth the way she had been doing. It was too confusing. Too dangerous.

The doll's face shone an unearthly white. It seemed to glow in the dim light as if lit from inside. As Meg stared at it the eyes seemed to be beyond tears. Not frightening or threatening anymore, just unbelievably sad. The doll looked defeated. As if it had failed. Then, almost as if somewhere, someone had flicked a switch, the glow faded and died.

Meg felt a pain in her chest. Was this what made people say their hearts were breaking? It only lasted a moment but it made her want to go back once more and see them all again. She knew now just how dangerous it was but she needed to. Just one more time. She picked up the doll and returned to bed.

"Sorry, Poss. You aren't going to like this." She pushed the heavy cat over, waiting for the hiss, the scramble, and the sound of him thudding onto the floor. Nothing happened.

It's time he got over that silliness, she thought, as she snuggled in between the cat and doll and went to sleep.

She was shocked when she woke up, the sun streaming in through the curtains. She was not in the cot in Fort Carlton. She was still in the bed at Grandma's. Beside her Poss stretched and yawned. The familiar room frightened her. Why was she still here?

Something was wrong! She stared at the doll. The eyes looked different. No, that wasn't it. That wasn't it at all. And that was what was wrong. The eyes didn't look different and they should. They had always seemed different: knowing, taunting, smug—so many expressions, and now they were just plain painted eyes—doll's eyes. And Meg had slept with Jessie and nothing had happened. Nothing.

Old Possum rubbed against her, purring. He walked across Meg. He stepped on Jessie. And kept on purring. Then he dropped to the floor and walked out of the room.

The doll was just a doll. Whatever she was before, Meg thought, she is just a doll now. Poss knows. She sat on the edge of the bed, her head in her hands. Empty. She felt empty.

"Poss says you're ready for breakfast!" Grandma was standing in the doorway, a tray in her hands. "I hope you're hungry."

Meg piled up the pillows. She couldn't let Grandma see how upset she was. And she realized she *was* hungry. She was surprised how hungry she was. She ate the two poached eggs on toast, drank her juice, and finished off the glass of milk as Grandma sat beside her looking pleased.

"Now you just stay there while I clear this tray away. I've got something to show you!"

Meg got out of bed. She wanted to be up, away from the bed which no longer seemed like a refuge.

"I'll come downstairs, it's . . . it's more cheerful in the kitchen."

She looked out of the window. It must have rained in the night. Grandma's garden sparkled in the sunlight. The paint on the old-fashioned swing glistened. She decided she'd go out for a while later so she dressed quickly.

Meg was surprised at how much better she felt. She'd been starving. But there was still an empty feeling. As if she'd lost something. Something she could never find again.

When she arrived in the kitchen, Grandma was sitting on the window seat with a pile of fat leather-bound books. Old albums. Meg curled up beside her, with Poss purring like a faulty motor on the other side.

"You wanted to know who you looked like, so I thought we could look through these old pictures of the Shearers and Camerons and see if there was anyone."

There were a lot of pictures. Starting with the Shearers and Starks in Peterborough County in the mid-eighteen hundreds. Everyone stood very formally, leaning on

115

dainty antique tables, or sat in elegant-looking chairs. Some of the older ladies sat, wearing funny caps and holding Bibles. They were decidedly on the heavy side. Meg didn't think they were a very lively looking lot and she was glad she didn't look like any of them.

"Cameras were new in those days and they had to make special trips to be photographed. All dressed up, of course, just like today, but in those days the film was slow-acting and they had to hold completely still for a long time. That's why they look so stiff and stuffy," Grandma explained.

Meg turned the pages. There were young couples. She supposed these were wedding pictures but the brides didn't wear fancy white dresses the way she'd always thought they did. The pictures were funny too in that the lady always stood, holding the back of the man's chair. And they generally looked angry or frightened or maybe a bit of both.

One of the couples had switched about. The lady was sitting and Meg realized that she looked familiar. She seemed to be nervous too but she was trying to smile, and if she had, the smile would have twinkled, Meg knew. And the man, standing very straight and proud and maybe a little fierce, was a younger Papa. Meg thought they looked very nice.

"Now, there's one I know. That's the wedding picture of your great-great-*great*-grandparents, Hannah and John Shearer, Meg."

Meg was almost afraid to turn the page. She waited, until finally Grandma reached across and did it for her.

"Now there! There they are with their little family. That was taken just before they left to come west. 1882 it was, I believe. They had their picture taken for the family back in Ontario. As a matter of fact they didn't get to a photographer again, not until the children were grown."

There they were! Meg gazed at the familiar faces. There was Mother sitting, holding Lizzie as if the child was about to take off at any moment. And she probably was, thought

Meg. Papa, looking very stern and wearing a funny high-buttoned suit, was sitting in front of a fancy carved mantlepiece or sideboard or something. Beside him, standing, chest out and shoulders back and looking very pleased with himself, was Archy. Geordie was half kneeling at Mother's side. No clown grin this time. He looked a little scared, as if he might actually cry.

And there *she* was. Morag. Sitting between her parents. Not wearing the plain blue flannel that Meg was used to, but dressed in an elegant old-fashioned dress with lace at the neck like Mother had, with bows down the front and ruffles on the skirt. Her face unsmiling—expectant. Holding Jessie, who was dressed in ruffles to match.

"Four children, the youngest not yet three, and they set off with only their few settlers' supplies to begin a new life." Grandma paused thoughtfully. "I used to think it was an ordeal to take your mother and the others to Saskatoon on the bus when they were little!"

Meg smoothed the picture. She didn't want Grandma turning the page just yet.

"Let's see. Archibald was the oldest. He was named after the first Shearer to come to Canada from Scotland. 1808 or thereabout. And Great-Uncle George. There were some stories about him, though he was an old man when I was born. The two girls. Your great-great-grandmother, of course and . . . well, isn't that strange? I can't think of the other girl's name . . ."

"Liz . . ." Meg started to say and then caught herself. "Let's . . . let's see if there are more pictures," she finished, feeling silly. "Maybe they'll have the names written underneath."

"Oh, I'll think of it," Grandma said. "It was a nice name. I always liked it." She turned the page.

I wouldn't care for a name like Lizzie, thought Meg, but then, it's probably short for Elizabeth. So Geordie grew up to be George. Her Great-Great-Great Uncle

117

George. She couldn't imagine him as an old man but she must get Grandma to tell her some of those stories.

There was a picture of Mother and Papa. Grey-haired, posing together again, not afraid or angry, but looking sad. Desperately sad.

"We had a big picture like that one," said Grandma, pointing to it, "that hung in our sitting room when I was a child. I always thought it was the saddest picture in the world. They had just found out she had cancer. She died not long afterwards."

Meg couldn't bear to look at the picture. She turned the page.

There were three studio portraits, two men and a woman. Meg recognized one right away. It was Archy. Older and much more dignified but still, she thought, with the same kind look in his eyes that she'd known. She pointed.

"That must be Archibald, right Grandma?"

"Yes, and there's George and . . ."

Meg couldn't hold back the giggles. He had a big, bushy mustache and where Archy had looked dignified, Geordie was trying to and, as far as Meg was concerned, not succeeding. She couldn't understand why she hadn't recognized him right away. He looked just like the young Geordie, bigger of course, wearing a false mustache and pretending to be grown up.

Her laughter was getting out of control. If only she could take that picture back and tease him with it. Wouldn't that be fun! And then she remembered. She couldn't go back and her laughter died.

"There she is," said Grandma, pointing to the round-faced lady, "your great-great-grandmother!"

Meg stared. Was that what she was going to look like when she got old? She looked pleasant enough. Really very friendly and nice. Jolly, Meg thought. Yes, she decided, there was a Santa Claus look about her. And she was definitely plump. If Morag ended up looking like that, I will too. She really couldn't believe her eyes.

"She was a wonderful woman, my granny, so good and loving." Grandma's voice was soft. "A very special person . . . Elizabeth Shearer . . ."

"Lizzie!" Meg blurted. A mixture of relief and astonishment filled her. Of course. She should have guessed. That would be Lizzie, the same round face and beaming smile. The chunky two-year-old had become a solid middle-aged lady.

"Why yes, Meg." There was surprise in Grandma's tone. "You're right! I always thought it was such a shame—she had a lovely name like Elizabeth and everyone called her Lizzie her whole life." She stared at Meg. "It's peculiar that you'd guess a thing like that!"

But another thought had struck Meg. But *she* wasn't my great-great-grandmother! Jessie wasn't *her* doll! She flipped the pages back. "Jessie belonged to . . . to the other girl."

Grandma looked at the photograph as Meg pointed. Her voice was gentle, hesitant. "Oh yes . . . I remember her name now. It was Morag. I suppose the doll was hers originally . . ." Grandma studied the family group. "Yes, she's holding it in that picture." She peered more closely at the picture. "I really need my glasses, the faces are so small . . ." Meg slid off the window seat and got the glasses from beside the phone.

"I suppose," Grandma said thoughtfully, "Jessie must have been given to my granny when they lost Morag."

"Lost her?" Meg was incredulous. Morag was found. Safe in the cot at Fort Carlton, with Mother . . . and Geordie.

Grandma sounded apologetic. "I guess that's just the old-fashioned way of talking about a child who never lived to grow up. To say they lost her." Grandma paused. "It was such a sad story, such a sad ending to their long trip west."

119

18

Meg didn't want to hear it but she knew she should know. And she needed to know.

She already knew most of it. The prairie fire. The two girls, not noticed until the wagon reached the fort, the North-West Mounted Policemen holding onto a frantic father and mother who wanted to run back into the flames to find their children.

"She managed to not only save her little sister from the fire, but kept her warm and safe that night in the cold rain. Of course, she wasn't strong, she'd been sick, and it was too much for her."

And now Meg understood. Why Jessie was just a doll again. Why she woke up here and not there, in Fort Carlton with Mother and Geordie. She should have known.

"She was a very brave girl." Grandma put on her glasses and leaned closer to the photograph. "My goodness, Meg! She looks just like you! Or maybe it should be you look like her . . . You do, indeed. That's who you take after . . . Angel Morag!"

"Angel Morag?"

Grandma laughed. "That's why I couldn't remember her real name. I always heard her called that—Angel

Morag. When I was little, I thought it was her name . . . one word . . . like Angeline or Angelica or something. Angelmorag! I suppose it was because I heard about it mostly from my granny and all she remembered of it was falling out of the wagon and her wonderful big sister coming to her rescue. Then, I suppose, they would have told her Morag had gone to be an angel when she died. A little one would take it literally, you know. Anyway, your Great-Great-Grandmother Lizzie always called her Angel Morag, so I did too." She reached over and gave Meg a hug. "I'm glad you're interested in knowing about your family history. They were special people and it's a shame they've been forgotten."

I won't forget them, thought Meg. Never.

Grandma closed the album. "I think we should go for a little drive. Get out into this beautiful day."

It sounded like a good idea to Meg. The fresh air felt wonderful, the sky an enormous dome of blue without a cloud in it. She breathed deeply, not wanting to get into the car.

Grandma came out loaded down with a pillow and blanket and a large paper bag. She laughed at Meg's questioning look. "That," she said, throwing the pillow and blanket into the back seat, "is in case you get tired." She waved the paper bag, ". . . and this, is in case *we* get hungry!"

Meg laughed. She peeked in the bag wondering what kind of lunch Grandma could have packed so fast. Two apples, two bananas, a whole box of crackers and a hunk of her favourite marbled cheddar cheese. "So, where are we going?" she asked as she fastened her seat belt.

"Oh, just a drive," but she sounded pleased about something.

They didn't talk. Most of the time Meg thought of the family, of how long it would have taken them to cover the ground the car was speeding over. Once she saw a bluebird flash along the road like a piece of stolen sky, and another time she saw a meadowlark sitting on a fencepost, the dark V bright against its yellow front. It looked as though it was singing but she couldn't hear anything inside the car. Sometimes it was better to be in a wagon.

"I thought you might like to see the old farm. Where I grew up, and the original homestead the Shearers settled on. You've never been there, have you?"

"No," said Meg. And she felt a sudden sorrow, knowing that she would never see it, with Mother and Lizzie . . . or Geordie.

"It's so different from when I was a child, I hardly come out anymore. You like to remember things the way they were." They drove along, Grandma pointing out the farms of different family members, some of them still being farmed by descendants of Archy and Geordie and Lizzie.

"Now, down this road's something that wasn't around when I was growing up." Grandma was driving down a wide road cut in a hillside. Below them, trees nearly filled the ravine, but above, the steep bank looked familiar, the prairie grass bleached and clinging.

Meg had a strange feeling of uneasiness. Almost fear.

"There it is, they've rebuilt Fort Carlton!"

Meg felt more than fear now. What was wrong? The fort was in the wrong place! Even counting that she'd only had a brief glimpse from the wagon, and that the old trail was up on top of the bank. Something was wrong.

Grandma parked the car and climbed out. Woodenly, Meg followed. Where had she been? Where had Morag been?

"Of course this isn't the fort the Shearers came to . . ."

Meg felt a surge of relief that faded just as quickly. Of course not—this was rebuilt.

"The fort that burned in 1885 during the Rebellion was over there." She pointed to an empty field. "When I was a little girl there were still hollows where the cellars had been. This is copied from plans of an earlier fort."

Meg felt much better. The fort she had seen had been exactly where Grandma pointed.

"Shall we go in and look around?" Grandma moved ahead.

Meg followed her. She was not sure she could have if it had been a reproduction of the real fort—Morag's fort. She would not have been able to go where she, where Morag had. . . . She would have been afraid of the memories, the feelings. But she followed Grandma, pretending to be interested.

They had lunch at some picnic tables nearby. Grandma pointed to the hill above them. "There are still the ruts from the old Carlton Trail up there. They must have been more than a foot deep when I was a girl. Maybe some day when you're feeling stronger we could climb up there."

I'd like that, thought Meg as they got into the car and drove away. She did not turn to look at the new fort.

"One last stop, if you feel up to it, Meg." Grandma drove past the former homestead.

Meg felt drowsy. The car was hot from sitting in the sunshine. She didn't want to think, anyway. She was almost dozing when she realized Grandma had pulled up in front of a small country church. She got out and began to walk up the path behind the church. Meg followed her.

"My granny used to take me up to the graveyard every Sunday after church. Some people have funny ideas about cemeteries but it was one of my favourite places. Every year she'd plant flowers so the plots were always blooming. She'd tell me stories about the different people." She laughed. "It seemed almost like a visit!"

Meg could see a double stone of pale granite. SHEARER and underneath, the names Hannah and John. Something written down below: *THO OUT OF SIGHT TO MEMORY DEAR.*

Grandma had moved on to some other tombstones with the Shearer name, but before Meg could read them she saw the small stone angel. It was the kind she had seen before on children's graves in country churchyards.

Morag Shearer
1872–1882

Grandma had come over and stood beside her now.

"That's another reason I always thought of her as Angelmorag, I suppose. My granny kept a rosebush planted here. What a shame—these saskatoon bushes are crowding in."

Meg was on her knees trying to read the fancy faded writing at the bottom. There was a grey feather lying by the stone and she used it to brush the dirt out of the letters. Gone But Not Forgotten, it said. Meg had seen that on lots of old tombstones, but this was the first time it meant anything.

They walked quietly back to the car.

"Where did you get that?" asked Grandma, pointing to the feather Meg still held.

"On the grave." Meg pointed back towards the statue.

"I think angels have white feathers," said Grandma, giving her a hug. "That looks like a seagull's."

Meg smiled. "I'm glad you brought me here . . . to see Morag's . . . Morag's angel."

"I'll never forget how surprised I was when I found out who'd bought that nice statue and had it put up . . . Great-Uncle George!"

Meg was not surprised Geordie would do that for Morag. He had done even more for Meg. She knew that now.

"I couldn't imagine him doing a thing like that. He was such a tease, even as an old man. He never behaved the way I thought an old man should. Why, one day when I was here with my granny . . ."

"Yes?" Meg wanted to speed her up.

"She was telling me about Angelmorag, and he came up

and . . . I was really shocked at what he said . . . I suppose he only said it to tease my granny, but still . . ."

Meg could hardly stand it. "What did he *say*, Grandma?"

"He said that the man who carved the angel wouldn't do it the way he wanted. He said if he'd done it right, it would have been the real angel Morag. He told us he'd asked the man to carve the angel winking!"

Meg felt a smile coming. "Winking!"

"Yes. Imagine, an angel with one eye winking!" She sounded almost as indignant as she must have felt all those years ago.

"The Clown," said Meg, her voice tender.

"And then . . . then the old scoundrel told us he thought Morag would have liked that! Imagine!" She slammed her car door as she got in.

As Meg opened the door on her side she caught a glimpse of her reflection in the window. For a moment Morag twinkled the smile back at her.

She looked back towards the angel. Softly, so that it would be drowned out by the motor starting, Meg murmured, "She would have. She would have liked it fine."

About the Author

Cora Taylor was born at Fort Qu'Appelle, Saskatchewan, and spent her childhood on her grandmother's farm near Carlton. In 1968 she returned to school to study English and took story-writing, play-writing, and film-writing courses under such masters as W. O. Mitchell and Rudy Wiebe. She has published several magazine articles, is the author of two musical plays, and has had her work broadcast on CBC Radio. She is actively involved with the Edmonton Branch of the Canadian Authors' Association, and was editor of the *Alberta Poetry Yearbook* from 1980 to 1987.

Cora is married to Russ Taylor and has four children, four stepchildren, and fourteen grandchildren. She currently raises goats, donkeys, rabbits, chickens, and dogs on an acreage just outside Edmonton.

The Doll is her second book written for children. Her first, *Julie*, won the Canada Council Children's Literature Prize, the 1985 Canadian Library Association's Book of the Year for Children Award, and the Alberta Writers' Guild R. Ross Annett Award for Children's Literature.